# AWAKEN YOUR INNER SELF

# PRAISE FOR THE AUTHOR

*The book beautifully covers the seen and unseen, the religion and spirituality, the call of duty, soul and Karma and the connect between God and man.*

**—Dr MJ Khan**

Chairman, ICFA

*These stories are on the essence of our existence, i.e., the Self minus ego. This is a book worth reading for seekers of Truth.*

**—Dr Girish Bapat**

Chairman, Mensa India & Director,
Jnana Prabodhini Institute of Psychology

*As he says, '… … … the 'perfume' of spirituality is the inner joy that you feel, the laughter that bubbles out of nowhere, the compassion, the sense of belonging with the Universe. You do not see or feel or smell the Real, but you experience its effects." This delightful perfume is amply evident in these stories..*

**—Iqbal Ali Khamis Al Lawati**

Author, Ex-Vice President, Central Bank of Oman

# AWAKEN YOUR INNER SELF

## STORIES FOR YOUR SOUL

KISHORE ASTHANA

An imprint of
Srishti Publishers & Distributors

**Srishti Publishers & Distributors**

A unit of AJR Publishing LLP

212A, Peacock Lane

Shahpur Jat, New Delhi – 110 049

editorial@srishtipublishers.com

First published by

Srishti Publishers & Distributors in 2024



10 9 8 7 6 5 4 3 2 1

This is a work of non-fiction, based on the authors' experiences and life-learnings. The views expressed in the book are the author's own and are not intended to hurt the sentiments of any individual, community, group, sect or religion.



Printed and bound in India.

*Dedicated to all the Masters who have guided me in lives past and continue to do so in the present one*

# Contents

*From the Spirit,*
*of the Spirit*

This is for those who are interested in the Spiritual and want to discover what lies ahead when they see religion in the rear-view mirror

## The Password

*When you reach the Beloved's door*
*Don't knock or call*
*I have been told*
*The password is soundless*

# Words

So many words in the world, spoken and unspoken. So much prose. Also, its stylish sister, poetry, aplenty. Some in search of closure, some for revenge, much for venting feelings, grave and otherwise. Some for power, some for pelf, some for ego that we think is our self.

So many songs in praise of God. So many recitals for the Divine, all seeking peace of one or other kind.

These are waves and eddies, in the clear ether of existence, flickering reflections, the kinetic, hiding the potential under the surface.

Only in absolute silence, when the surface is calm, the Truth of us, the Haq that we are, shimmers, and, beyond ideas and concepts, beyond words, uttered & unuttered, we find bliss.

❧

**And yet, this silence speaks sometimes, and when it does, here is some of what it says. This is a pale shadow of what it feels like to be there, but this still carries some of its divine fragrance.**

❧

# You & Me

*Beyond shape and size, large and small, unaffected by water, earth or fire, I am nothing. I am all without attachments, without desire. In silence I sit with those, the few who understand. No prophet am I, no God, just a son of this ancient land.*

*I go back to my ancestors, knowing, calm and wise. As they were, so am I, just my Self—no surprise. I am not what you see, this fleeting body, fickle mind. I am not my hopes and fears; I have left those behind.*

*Shorn of all that I am not, like the sun in a cloudless sky, in the quiet of the Self, this eternal soul am I. An eddy in the ocean, I am well-defined, but the ocean is true. Pure gold in ornaments fine—that I am, and so are you.*

# The Lover & the Boatman

I was one with my beloved, but we parted suddenly, I still do not know why. One day, when I was near a wide river, I saw my beloved waiting for me on the other shore. I waded into the river, but realized that the river was too deep, and I could not cross it without help.

As I looked around, a boat approached me. It stopped near me, and a ladder was dropped. The boatman greeted me as I climbed aboard and said, "I see that you are trying to cross the river. Come with me. I will help you."

Days passed, and the boatman plied me with many things. There were fruits of all kinds – apples were there in plenty, and grapes. The boatman called the apples 'malum'. It was only later that I learnt that this was also the Latin word for 'evil'. But, by that time, it was too late. I was truly hooked on to the comforts, and the food and wine were intoxicating. I even ignored the fact that the boat kept sailing downstream and not across the river.

I had long discussions with the boatman. He called himself Khewaiyya. Prompted by an inner voice, I once asked him when we would reach the other shore. To my great surprise, he said, "Never! I am in love with you, and I want to stay with you forever."

This made me pause. Yes, the boatman was caring, and my mind felt flattered. However, my heart kept whispering that my real beloved was on the other shore, and even though we kept sailing downstream, in quiet moments I could still see him as, faithfully, he kept pace with us. Unfortunately, I liked dancing to the boatman's songs, and his music made me look the other way most of the time.

I meditated often, for the sight of the beloved, even though rare, made my heart become still. During these meditations, I contemplated jumping into the river and swimming across. The boatman must have sensed this, for he said, "Do not even think about it. The river is deep and the current strong. You will surely die."

Finally, the boatman stopped at a dock. I disembarked, and after a brief rest on the shore, climbed onto another boat. Unfortunately, the same story was repeated here. The boatman called himself Kevat this time. There was a third boat at the next stop, and then a fourth and a fifth. I met Majhi, Chuanfu, Barciaolo, Ruderer, Varkaris, Sendo, Naviscompleo, Mallah and many more. Soon I lost count. I became a habitual traveller, changing boats at docks where my current boat stopped when its journey was over. Throughout, I remained on this side of the river.

During the large number of boat-rides, I learnt many things and matured. Some older boatmen showed me miracles. After a while, I found that I could perform some miracles, too. However, I realized that these were just *karāmāt* – small miracles born of some spiritual powers and not miracles, *mu'jizāt*. These seemed to make the boatmen appear more powerful, but I did not want to become involved in *siddhis* and I ignored these.

Then, during deep introspection one day on the deck of my latest boat, I felt very close to my beloved. He was still on the other shore for sure, but I could feel his presence inside me. I asked myself how I could make this presence permanent. The answer came unbidden – "You have to steer your boat yourself." But what to do about the boatman? True, I had noticed that he had become quite weak, but he was still in charge. To my shock, the voice inside me said, "Kill him."

That evening, while I was lighting the lamps, the boatman came by and started inspecting a damaged side rail near me. On an impulse, I suddenly pushed him into the river. He used to be a good swimmer but was weak now and kept splashing around, pleading to help him back up.

Out of curiosity, I asked him, "All the other boatmen told me their name. You didn't. Who are you?"

"We boatmen all have the same name," he said, "regardless of what others have told you."

"And what is this name?" I asked.

Before he sank out of sight, he shouted, "Ego."

With the boatman dead, something very surprising happened. Entirely on its own, the boat started moving towards the other shore.

I smiled. I could see my beloved smiling, too.

*And now, on the other shore, not for me pilgrimages galore, or visits to seers, door to door. Wherever I look, there I am. My holy land is where I am.*

## For My Fellow Sailors, My Journey Thus Far

*I started my voyage years back, where the ocean was dark and deep*
*Many monsters tried to drown me, I've sent them to the deep*
*There were storms off and on and still waters, too*
*But I have learnt aplenty, on this ocean blue*

*I had come with a map, but lost it on the way*
*When my ego on the tiller led me astray*
*I made many wrong turns, but that's in the past*
*Now my Guru's flag flies on my mast*

*Having fended off krakens, having muted the siren's song*
*Now I see land ahead, where I truly belong*
*I'll sail my boat wisely, till I reach that welcome shore*
*Where those I loved, are waiting for me by the door*

*Other boats will follow, with those I hold dear*
*Who still have knots left, on this ocean here*
*Our boats are not the same but we sail together, true*
*And the home we return to, is the same for me and you*

*But let's laugh together meanwhile, life's given us this boon*
*Till we meet on our home-world, to sail again soon*
*For there's still much to learn, that only here can we find*
*In these very fragile boats, donning our body and mind*

*I'll journey with you next, on some voyages more*
*Till I realize in my being, and am entirely sure*
*That all is One, and the Trinity, isn't really Three*
*We are the Creator and the Creation, not just You and Me!*

# The Inner 'Lotus', That Is and Isn't

*A lesson in our Himalayan village*

It was the month of Aashvin, with Dussehra in a few days. The autumn morning breeze was cool in our small Himalayan village. Fifteen of us sat on the ground in a half circle around the Master after our morning yoga and light breakfast.

True Masters 'speak' through their silence, and our Master is one such. An aura of calm pervades his presence, and his bright eyes speak volumes. There is always a gentle smile on his face, and, as usual, we found ourselves mirroring it this morning, too.

As I looked at him, I thought that it must be so nice to be in 'his' serene universe. He was looking somewhere else but, as this thought struck me, he slowly turned to look straight into my eyes, smiled, and said, "My universe is your universe, too."

His direct gaze and his words 'flipped' something in my mind. To my surprise, for no discernible reason, I burst out laughing. The Master laughed, too. The others looked somewhat startled, but no one said anything for a while. Then, my friend, Kotu, always the naughtiest, grinned widely, happy at my happiness and asked, "Master, why did you and Auman laugh?"

"There are some things, Kotu, that no one can explain to another," the Master said, looking at him.

"I do not understand, Master. You laughed too, so you know why Auman laughed. Why can you not tell us why you laughed?" Kotu said.

"Let me show you why I cannot explain that to you, Kotu," the Master replied, pointing at the pond. "All of you, go, smell any lotus there and come back."

Our ashram is on the banks of a small mountain lake where white and pink lotus flowers bloom. All of us got up to go, but the Master motioned at me to sit down. The others ran to the pond as if it was a race, and the Master chuckled.

We kept sitting in silence for some time and then, as if sensing my unspoken question, he said, "I wanted you to wait here because we need them to speak to you when they return."

Soon I heard footsteps behind me and, as the others returned, the Master waved at them to sit. Once they had settled down, he asked, "Kotu, did you smell the lotus?"

Kotu nodded, and the Master said, "Describe the perfume to Auman."

Kotu eagerly turned to me and started speaking. "It was… it was… like… "

"Like a flower?" the Master prompted, and Kotu said, "Yes, yes, it was flowery."

"And?" the Master asked.

"Somewhat powdery. It was very soft-smelling, mellow…"

The Master turned to Aman and asked him to describe to me what the smell of a lotus flower was like. Aman had a slight case of sniffles. He said, "Master, I could not smell anything."

The Master told others to do the same, and each had his own description. They were all similar and full of similes. However, none was specific, and no two were exactly the same.

"Let us think about what has just happened. All of you experienced the same fragrance, but not everyone felt the same sensation. Aman could not even sense anything," the Master said. "It was the same with our laughter just now. It was the emanation of the inner lotus that Auman and I shared. Auman's experience was similar to mine, but it was not the same. Like you know what a lotus smells like, but cannot describe the exact sensation of the fragrance to another, the perfume of the inner lotus has to be experienced and cannot be explained to another. Do you understand now, Kotu?"

"Yes, Master," Kotu nodded and asked, "when will I be able to experience the inner lotus?"

"Aman has a cold. He could not smell the lotus because his sense of smell has been compromised by a virus. Similarly, all of us have this virus that stops us from experiencing the inner lotus. It is called our ego."

"Do not misunderstand me – the ego is essential for our survival. However, when it is very strong, it overwhelms the mind and invades the heart. Then it becomes like a lid on your spiritual lotus, and you cannot sense it. However, you still experience many other things that give you joy and grief and that keeps you from thinking about your inner lotus."

"Like a rose!" Kotu blurted out.

"Yes, like a rose," the Master said, "a wonderful perfume, but not the same as that of a lotus. It leaves one with a sense of luxury, even decadence."

"What of jasmine, Master?" someone else asked.

"Another very nice fragrance," the Master said, "we can imagine strings of these flowers in the hair of ladies."

"Marigolds remind me of temples," Aman said, "they have a nice perfume too."

"Yes, marigolds remind me of rituals, too," the Master said, "another pleasant fragrance."

Anand, who was the quietest amongst us, said, "There are bad smelling flowers, too. I have heard that there are some flowers that smell like rotting meat."

"Ah, yes, the Rafflesias are one such. Like their smell, we also have bad experiences now and then," the Master said. "It is up to us to ensure that we react calmly to them." He paused and then continued, "By the way, do you know why these flowers smell like rotting meat?"

"No," someone said.

"They smell like that because they want to attract flies which pollinate them. You see, the carrion flower knows how to use the flies. In your life, you will also meet many who will spread lures for you, offering things that tempt you. If you fall for any of these temptations, they will use you, and you will stray from the Path."

We were silent for a while, absorbing this. Then the Master resumed, "Let us get back to our nicer flowers. Spirituality is not the perfume of the marigold or rose or jasmine. Each of these is a beautiful, aromatic flower and all of us have our own associations for each of these."

The Master added softly, "Spirituality is not even the subtle fragrance of the lotus."

After a short pause, he said somewhat firmly, "Enough similes. None of these represent the spiritual lotus in your spiritual heart, which itself is a 'lotus' only in name. The spiritual heart is not a physical organ, and the spiritual lotus is not a physical flower."

"What do you mean, Master? There is no spiritual lotus?" I asked.

The Master chuckled, "Similes are merely examples and not real. The 'real' has no shape, form, substance or aroma, but we can only describe it in terms that our senses are familiar with. That is why no description can ever suffice, and my own Master never encouraged anyone to describe what the 'real' felt like."

"If it is so shapeless, formless, perfume-less, how do we ever experience it?" Anand asked.

"Our physical senses are not needed for this experience," the Master said, "If you smell a flower in a room, you do not need to see or touch the flower to know that the flower is there. Similarly, the 'fragrance' of spirituality is the inner joy that you feel, the laughter that bubbles out of nowhere, the compassion, the sense of belonging with the Universe. You do not see or feel or smell the Real, but you experience its effects."

"And then what happens?" Anand asked.

"Then, as always, it depends on you. If you continue to travel the path of wisdom till its end, this divine fragrance becomes a permanent part of you and you become a permanent part of it. You start living in the Universe that made us laugh."

"So, Auman is living there now?" Kotu asked, looking at me, grinning quizzically.

The Master laughed and said, "Not quite just now, Kotu, but he was a visitor here for a short while, and has seen the joy that pervades all. One day, he may even stay here permanently. You may do so, too."

The Master paused, smiled and said, "I hope that now you know the difference between the actual flower and the real lotus, so when I say, 'Wake up and smell the lotus' I do not want you all rushing to the lake this time."

All of us laughed. The Master got up and so did we. It was time for our meditation.

# At the Necropolis of the Gods

*Death is an evil. That's what the gods think or they would die. – Sappho*

But, Sappho, these gods are the ones who have shed their mortal coil and, in our terms, have already 'died'. When we die, we, too, will reach their realm. Do see what I found when I visited them there.

Last night I visited the necropolis of the gods. It came about because I was thinking about the idea that the gods are immortal and would not need a place to bury their dead, and I just wanted to confirm it. However, to my surprise, I found that they did have such a place and, not only that, they guarded it fiercely. I had no idea whose remains I would find there and was surprised at what I saw.

I will come to that, but it was not as simple as just visiting the place and asking for directions. Fortunately, I had a guide who was very helpful.

Let me start from the beginning. That itself was unexpected. I found myself on the shore of a river, so wide that I could not see the other shore. There was a pier and a bell. I rang the bell, and from a distance, I saw a boat approach. "Ah," I said to myself, "that must be Charon, coming to take me across. This must be the river Styx."

When the boatman came closer, I could see that he was not at all like the frightening images I had seen of Charon. "Are you Charon?" I asked him.

"Everyone who comes here asks me that," he replied, "I am getting somewhat tired of answering this question."

"No, and I am not Hermes either, and before you ask, this river is not called Styx or Acheron."

"You are in the Kalunga line. This is the boundary between the world of the living and the dead, as people in your Congo knew. In fact, in Kikolongo, Kalunga means 'the threshold between worlds'.

"Alright," said I, "and you are?"

"You will find out who I am when you return," he said, and added with a somewhat strange look, "if you return."

"At least tell me why you ferry people across this divide," I said.

"Because someone has to," he said, "and who better than me?"

So, he wants to give me no answers, I thought. Never mind. At least he will take me across.

"Step in," said he, "but remember, hardly any who do so need my services to return."

"But some do, for sure?"

"Yes," he said. "Some do. These are either very advanced souls for whom this river boundary does not exist, or, in a few rare cases, they are genuinely curious ones like you, who have a strong sense of the self."

I stepped into the boat and saw him clearly for the first time. He was a young man, without a beard, and looked quite fit. He looked at me and smiled.

"Why do you want to visit the city of the gods?" the boatman asked.

"I have always wanted to confirm whether the gods are immortal," I said.

"And how do you plan to do so?" the boatman asked.

"On my plane, every town and village has a place where they bury or cremate their dead. We even have some ancient 'cities' where only the dead are buried. I want to see if the city of gods has such a place. If it doesn't, I will know that they are immortal."

"That's the first time I have heard this reason for a quest like yours," the boatman said, smiling again. “Most come to meet the gods of their choice or to confirm that the gods really exist.”

“And do they?” I asked. “Do they exist, I mean.”

“You will see for yourself,” he said somewhat cryptically.

There was no sense of time in the crossing. In the blink of an eye, or so it seemed to me, we were on the other shore. As I disembarked, I found a young woman standing there to greet me.

“Welcome,” she said. “I am Abeona, the goddess of outward journeys. I am one of the Chimata-no-kami.”

“Chimata what?” I said, somewhat distracted by the light surrounding her.

“Chimata-no-kami,” she said, “we are a band of spirits who guide travellers.”

“Thank you for coming to guide me,” I said, truly grateful.

“I sense that you want to visit the necropolis of the gods? Yes, we do have a necropolis here, but not exactly like you may have imagined.”

I must have looked surprised, for she added, “Oh, we communicate telepathically here and the boatman sent me his thoughts well before you arrived.”

“Yes,” said I, “can you guide me there?”

“Of course,” she said, “I have sent a message to Mara – You may know him as Yama, who is responsible for the spirits after death. The attendant at the necropolis, Ankou, has been told to show you around.”

“Come,” she said and walked away, with me closely behind her.

“We will have to go through the city of gods to reach there,” Abeona said. “Just don’t start dawdling there. So many have got lost and never returned.”

“No, I have a lot waiting for me back home,” I said, “and I do not want to disturb any of the gods here, anyway.”

Abeona smiled.

We walked through beautiful roads and soon we were in a large round open area with a clock tower in the centre. I noticed that this clock tower had no clock. I asked Abeona about this and she said, "There is no clock because time does not exist in the city of gods."

"I do not understand," I said.

"This is one of those things that you will have to experience to understand. No one can explain it to you before that," Abeona replied.

"Why do you have the clock tower, then?" I asked.

Abeona smiled, "If the tower was not there, would you have asked about time?"

"Perhaps not!" I said.

"This is why the clock tower is there. It emphasizes that time does not matter here."

Abeona pointed to the area and explained, "This is the centre of the city of gods." This city is built in a wheel and spoke pattern with roads going outwards from the centre. Each road is reserved for one kind of god. There are roads for gods of creation, gods of destruction, moon gods, sun gods, gods of the earth, gods of water, air, fire, of rivers, rain, storm, the sky and so on. There is a road also for humans who have become godlike. Some of them keep visiting your plane off and on."

"Do these gods get along with their neighbours?" I asked with a smile.

"Oh, they are essentially the same as their neighbours. Their houses are different only for visitors such as you, so that you can recognize them from your own cultural lores."

I saw one street sign which looked interesting.

"What's that?" I asked Abeona.

"Oh, that is the sign for the street of the creation gods. This is the sign of Nye Gyama. He who knows and sees everything."

"I see," I said.

"Yes, he has a house on the road for the gods of the sky, too," Abeona said.

Abeona told me stories about some of the gods as we passed their houses. I will not repeat them here because I am writing this about the necropolis of the gods, and I do not want to digress. However, I must mention that I was especially struck by the story of Niu Lang and Zhi Nu, the god and goddess of love, that Abeona told me as we passed a house where beautiful robes were hanging in the window.

"These are all woven by Zhi Nu," Abeona said. "She is the goddess of weaving for the gods and daughter of Shang Di, the supreme god. Zhi Nu, the goddess, and Niu Lang, the human, were star-crossed lovers. They were separated by the stars that Shang Di threw to stop Niu Lang from following Zhi Nu; stars that you call the Milky Way. Now the poor lovers can meet only once a year when magpies fly from earth to the Milky Way and form a bridge. Then Niu Lang and Zhi Nu go across to be with each other on the evening known as the Seventh Night of the Seventh Moon."

I found some houses specially adorned with flowers and lights. Abeona explained that when humans celebrate a special day for a god, that god recognizes the celebration and reflects it in his abode.

We finally reached a gate and Abeona said, "This is our necropolis. You will find no gods buried here as gods do not die, even when humans stop believing in them. Can you imagine the sun, the moon, the sky, rain, rivers, etc. dying if you stop believing in them? No, they live on here, with their namesakes, and to be met by occasional visitors such as you."

"Then who is buried here?" I asked.

"You will see," Abeona said. "I must leave now, as I am not allowed inside the necropolis. No gods can enter here, but you are no god, and you are allowed."

She turned, paused and turned back to say, "My partner, Adiona, will be here to guide you back. Be nice to her. She is the goddess of safe return."

And she was gone.

I rang the bell and a shadowy figure wearing a black coat and large hat shuffled towards the gate from inside and opened the gate with a clang.

"Come..." Ankou said, gesturing to me with a skeletal finger.

I could not quite see his face and, for the first time, felt trepidation at my enterprise. However, it was too late to do anything about it and so I followed.

"Why are gods not allowed here?" I asked Ankou on the way.

"Well, you see, what we have buried here is what they had to give up to become gods," Ankou said in his gruff voice. "Despite what you may have heard in various stories made by humans who think that the gods are in their own mental and physical image; all the gods in the city of gods are truly sublime. We do not want any of them to come and risk being tempted by any of these things that we have buried here."

I could hardly contain my surprise, but Ankou would say no more.

We eventually came to a large building. Ankou opened the solid-looking door with a key that was as big as my arm. As the door swung open, golden lights came on inside. We entered and the door slowly sealed behind us. I looked back and saw that there was no door knob, key hole or anything else that could open the door from inside. I shivered slightly.

I looked inside and saw that there were sealed golden caskets all over the huge room, arranged in neat rows. On each was a name engraved in English and Hindi.

"Why these two languages?" I asked Ankou.

"Because you can read them," Ankou said. When someone comes who can read Arabic or Japanese, the names will be in Arabic or Japanese. It works for everyone.

"Do many visitors come here?" I asked.

"No. However, those you consider seers on earth come to deposit what they have given up. You are the only one who has come out of curiosity."

I went through some rows, reading the labels. I saw the caskets of Anger, Envy, Sloth, Slyness, Greed, Pride, Lust, Delusion and many other such things.

"Satisfied?" Ankou asked after I had seen about one fifth of these caskets.

"Yes," I said.

"Do you understand?" Ankou asked.

"I think I do," I said. "The gods have given up all these to become gods. Yes, I do."

"You, too, can give up these and become a God, if you wish," Ankou said, "but only if you are ready. Not everyone is."

"I am not ready," I told Ankou, "but one day I will be."

"Come again when you are," Ankou said. "Let us go now. I can sense Adiona waiting for you outside."

We came out of another door at the back, which opened by itself when we approached. There was a niche in the wall just before the exit. I was curious to see what was in it. I went closer and saw there an ornate casket, much bigger than the rest. On it was written, **EGO**, in bold letters.

Ankou read my thoughts and said, "All who want to be gods must surrender their ego here. If you want to keep your ego, you cannot become a God."

"But we have so many stories about gods feeling insulted and vengeful. Is that not their ego acting up?"

"As you say, they are stories. You can make up any story you want and you humans tend to be very imaginative!" Ankou said.

"Some stories have a germ of truth in them, but almost all are merely ones in which humans have imbued the gods with their own biases and qualities," Ankou continued.

As I was thinking about what Ankou had said, he spoke again, "Do you think the wind is angry when it becomes a storm? Do you think the fire is vengeful when it burns? Do you think that the earth is fearful when it trembles? No, the god of wind or of fire or of earth have no such emotions. They act as they must."

Ankou paused and continued, "It is the same with all the gods. They act as they must. One day, you will realize this, too."

"Hmm ...," I said and thought – another thing that I must experience to understand. I asked, "Why have you put this casket at the end?"

"It becomes easier to surrender the ego when you have surrendered the rest," Ankou said.

"But if we surrendered our ego first, wouldn't all else come automatically?" I asked.

"When the time comes, you will find that your ego is not so easy to get rid of. You may become loving, compassionate, calm, without anger or lust, but the ego remains alive and well."

I was reflecting on this experience as we exited the building and the door closed softly behind us and said, "I will definitely think about that."

Ankou gave me a smile that was less grim than his usual one and we moved around the building to the front gate of the necropolis, where I found Adiona standing. Like Abeona, she was wearing a white robe and there was an aura of light around her.

I thanked Ankou and greeted Adiona with folded hands and bowed head. She smiled and returned my greeting. We walked mostly in silence. On the way, Adiona said, "Did you learn anything from your visit here?"

"Yes, I did," I said, "I learned so many things. Most of all, I learnt that I am not ready to become a God, as yet."

Adiona gave a chuckle, and I added, "I also learned how kind all gods are, even Ankou, who tends to the necropolis. As are you and Abeona, helping a stranger like me."

"Oh, Abeona and I are always there to teach children not to fear during their journey through life. You are a child here, and we cannot but help you."

As we neared the pier, I asked Adiona, "Why did I not see any gods? Do they always keep inside their houses?"

"You did not see any gods because you did not come here to see them. If you had, they would have been here for you," Adiona replied.

When we reached the pier, I saw the now familiar boatman there. He smiled at me and waved, asking me to step on the boat. I thanked Adiona and the boatman, and we started our journey back. I was silent, trying to take in everything that I had seen and heard. The boatman was quiet, too.

When we reached the other shore, I stepped on the pier and turned to thank him. The boatman smiled and said, "Before you go, do you want to learn one more thing?"

"Of course," I said instantly.

"There is no river and no boat between your plane and where you have been. You see the river and the boat only because you expected to see a river and a boat. If you had not, we would not be here. No. There is no Charon, no Styx, no Acheron. In truth, Kalunga, the threshold between the worlds is only in your mind."

"Oh!" I said, surprised, "so I have imagined all this?"

"Some of it, yes," the boatman said. "The necropolis is real, of course. The city of gods, too. Both in a way not understood on your plane. Maybe one day we will find you here."

"Thank you for everything," I told the boatman with folded hands and turned to go.

"Don't you want to know who I am?" the boatman called behind me.

"Of course, I do!" I said, eagerly.

I turned around and drew a deep breath of surprise. There was no river, no boat and no boatman. Instead of the river, I saw a beautiful green meadow. Where the boatman and the boat had been, there was a large mirror.

# When I Dance

So many people dance with their bodies. They feel free and joyous and full of energy and pep. Many feel a sense of peace.

I have seldom danced with my body but, nevertheless, I dance frequently. I dance with my mind and its repertoire is immense.

I look at the love of my life and my mind dances the beautifully romantic Georgian Kartuli. Her softness and grace dance in my mind in close harmony with my love for her. Just she and I are there in this dance; she the only woman in the world for me, and I the only man in the world for her, during these magic moments.

Depending upon the mood, this lasts for some time. Often, she smiles at me, and my mind bursts forth in the colourfully energetic Acharuli, whirling around her in flashy attire, laughing with her laughing at me.

Sometimes I pause and thank my stars that my mind does not have to dance the Baba Karam, since I am no slave ruing his unattainable love for a princess. In my mind, I am the prince.

When I am in my logical moments, the mind dances the technically perfect south Indian Bharatanatyam. It dances to ancient beats, celebrating the beauty of the physical form, the beauty of numbers or words and finding the divine in these. I return from this performance elevated and happy at the perfection of my mind's movements; the pure logic which drives it ever forward.

The mind changes colours more than even the sea does. It segues from logic to fiction, from Bharatanatyam one moment to Kathak, donning dancing bells and dancing to wonderful stories, old and new, real and yet to be. During this dance, the mind wears a swirl of ideas and dances in free form, like my ancestor storytellers did physically. Sometimes the mind dances to a ghazal, at others, to a thumri. Sometimes, even to a bhajan. In introspective moments it may just dance to none of these but just show *bhaavs*, miming my various moods.

When this dance ends, I often notice a new story lying on the backdrop of my mind, shining like a gem in the sand. Sometimes it is just a few lines of poetry, telling the story of my heart, at others it is a longer one, telling the story of some others who live there.

And so, on it goes, dancing energetic African dances or Chinese Lion dances or one of the many others from all over the world. I watch all these, sometimes with wonder and at others, with amusement. Some of the more acrobatic dances make me smile, some others make me laugh and yet others make me ponder life.

I have not found my mind dancing the dance of the whirling dervishes. It did not need this dance to arrive here; but, of course, other dances were needed, because you see, without these dances, life is meaningless and no progress is possible.

Yes, I am a dancer, too. It is just that my dances are different from the conventional; though full of what makes each dance so unique, creative and joyful. Sometimes, however, that is not enough, and the heart expresses its yearning thus:

> *Beloved, let me whirl in your heart, tonight, as you have done so long in mine. Keep your door ajar for though I know what you're like, inside me, I am dying to see if I am the same inside you!*

❧

# Me

## *A Visiting Scholar from Another Universe*

Not all aliens have weird features and eerie tentacles. Take me, for instance. I may be unusual but in a different way.

I exist in two universes simultaneously. One is the Purush universe, where I have come from, and yet, where I still am. (Yes, this is possible in our quantum universe.) The other is the Prakriti universe, which I have come to, as a visiting scholar for a short while. The quantum superposition collapses here, and I become objectified.

I have no labels in the Purush universe. I have no colour, no sex, no religion, no nationality, no name. I cannot be classified in any species. I have no form and can take any form. There I am pure Being with my own identity in the infinite, akin to a small iceberg floating in an ocean, waiting to melt and become one with it.

I have come to the Prakriti universe to study, many times over centuries, in different countries, and different nationalities, sometimes as a man, at others as a woman. I have been rich and poor here, in different lifetimes and have come here as brown, black, red, white or yellow over the aeons. One must have all kinds of experiences to take back to and evolve in the Purush universe.

As a visiting scholar in the Prakriti universe, I wear many identification labels. My name, nationality, religion, sex, species, domicile, colour, height, weight, financial status, academic degrees, etc., are all attributes that I am defined by and, in a sense, separated because of, from most others. This is essential here in Prakriti university to help other scholars recognize me, address me, assess me and interact with me. However, this onslaught of identities is so overwhelming that, sometimes, I forget that I am merely visiting here to learn something that cannot be learnt any other way. I call myself *jiva* and think I am an integral part of this Prakriti universe. I tend to doubt anyone who says anything to the contrary and fiercely defend the labels defining me here.

This happens more often when the Prakriti university curriculum tends to overwhelm, and *rajas,* the active passion, and *tamas,* the sloth, cloud over *sattva,* the purity and knowledge that I came here for. Then, full of emotions, I tend to forget that all these exist merely in my mind and are not a part of my real identify. In my attachment to the sensory attractions of the Prakriti universe, I do not remember that I will leave this baggage behind, along with my temporary body-mind, that I energize with my life-spark, when this term ends here.

I am alert for such moments because it is important to remain aware, in truth, that I am not this body-mind motivated by sattva, rajas and tamas. I must always be conscious that I am not a permanent part of the Prakriti universe. I am a visitor from the Purush universe, temporarily dwelling in the Prakriti universe that has been created for my evolution through learning that can only be obtained through life-experiences here. I am just one of so many other scholars who have all come here for an interactive group session this life around. Whenever I can, I still my mind and go behind the veil that hides the portal to the Purush universe. I enter there and become one with who I really am, beyond this scholar's garb that I wear as my body-mind. There I am aware of myself as the user of my consciousness and not its evident forms.

This foray into the Purush universe is not easy to achieve. My gurus have been generous enough to shower their grace on me and show me the way. Without their intervention, I do not think I could ever escape the control of my mind. The ego that it uses to keep me here is stricter than any university proctor.

During my brief forays in the Purush universe, I am who I am, and all is as it should be. I rest here in blissful calm awhile, before returning to the Prakriti university, as I must, till I 'graduate'. Life awaits there, with all its cacophony but this experience is essential since I still have courses I must take here.

All is not lost. When I return to the Prakriti universe, I bring something from my brief stay in my real abode. The residual effect of the harmony and coherence there fills my heart with calm and compassion. It sometimes manifests itself as unbidden laughter bubbling up from the centre of my being.

By curbing the ego somewhat, this residual feeling from the Purush universe also imbues the mind with a certain naïvete. Sometimes this can be exploited by the venal but, by and large, the feeling spreads an aura of calm and, with the benefit of its perspective, makes studying here tolerable.

So I live here in the Prakriti universe, doing what I must and learning all that I can. Some of my courses are pre-selected by me before coming here, keeping in mind what I need to learn this time around. Some others are decided upon by my will and a few thrusts upon me by other students. I try to take all with equanimity and, with a few exceptions, I am successful in doing so.

Like any other student, I look forward to my graduation. Then I can return to my Purush universe for good. I know that it is always there, waiting for me with its welcome embrace. The above ideation is akin to what is called Sankhya by scholars. Sankhya is an extensive philosophy with many explanations and many labels and sub-labels. That way lies the mesh of knowledge that entangles the explorer in ego driven epistemology and makes it more difficult, if not impossible, to visit the Purusha universe. I prefer to just remain with the simple concept of the Prakriti universe, wherein exists the university that I am currently attending, and the Purush universe where I come from and where my real home is. I urge you to do so, too; for too much knowledge is even more of an obstruction on this path as compared to too little knowledge.

# Why I Laugh When They Ask, "What Is Your Religion?"

Who am I, they ask, am I a Hindu, Muslim, Sikh or Isai? When I say nothing, they nudge me and say, "It is a simple question. Why don't you reply?"

Even if I wanted to, what can I say?

They sit proudly in their painted chariots. They have definite maps and revered charioteers. Their chariots have specific names, destinations and symbols painted on them. They do not get off their chariots, and they shun those in other chariots. They are all certain that their lord, who is their witness, has so ordained.

I am not on any chariot and that confuses so many looking down on me from their perches. More so, because they see me without a care, without fear of death, or even of living. My seemingly causeless laughter annoys them. They also dislike it when those who get off their chariots are greeted by me with a smile and an embrace.

Secretly, they envy me because they want to be like me but they cannot get down from their chariots. It is a sin, you see, to disagree with the charioteers and refuse to travel on the path they have laid out. It is a sin, often punishable by death, or at least by being promised to be sent to that horrible place called 'hell'. So, they will not come down to me. As I will not climb on to their chariots, there is little chance of them understanding me. What can I tell them then?

They do not remember a simple truism. If they continue on the path they are on, they will end up where their path takes them. The destination is not where they need to go but the vision espoused by the charioteers keeps them on a narrow road hemmed between fear and hope. Anyone who tries to show them reality is banished from the chariot. Sometimes, such nay-sayers are killed.

They don't understand me, but I understand them all too well for I have been, turn by turn, in all their chariots. I have pored over their maps and, realizing where they were headed, I have refused to go along with them. However, every time I have learnt something from my foray to help me along. I needed this learning for, once, I had a carriage, too – even though it was nothing like these labelled chariots.

Vedanta showed me the path. From the Guru Granth Sahib, I filled the gaps. I made bridges from the words of the Gospels and the Quran. From the ancient wisdom of the Dhammapada and Zend Avesta, I got the guiding instruments.

My carriage moved to the cadence of mystic mantras. The call of the aza'an and the sound of psalms played a role, too, as did the raag of the bairaagi. Encouragement from Sufi saints made my wheels go around. The light in my carriage came from Shirdi and Arunachal and from many other places.

The driver of my carriage was my inner voice, my Satguru. Even before I was born, we were close, and we remained so. Now that I am very near my destination, I do not need the carriage any more. The path has ended at the door.

So, even if I wanted to reply, what can I say? How can I make them realize that what they seek exists in silence and not in the din of their chariots? That their fears and hopes are illusory? How can I explain where my carriage has gone? How can I convince them that I have no use for the tuft of hair on a shaven head or a certain cap or beard or special attire?

And yet, I AM.

And, where I am, there is no need for all these things. There are no moral judgments. There is no heaven or hell, no rivers of milk or honey, no flaming devils, no judgmental Lord sitting on a throne, no crowns of gold or thorns. And, yes, even no 'life' or 'death'. Just I – and that's All There Is.

And that, my friends, is what makes me laugh. This laughter is no ordinary one. It bubbles up unbidden from the centre of my being and pervades all.

# Language of the Masters

Let me tell you about the language of the Masters. It is like nothing else in the universe. It is our natural heritage, yours and mine. In it are clues about where we have come from and who we are. It has no name. For the moment, for convenience, I will call it 'my language'. It is just a phrase. Deep down, this language is yours, too.

My language was once spoken the world over amongst women and men of goodwill. It has soft syllables and long pauses, pregnant with possibility. It is spoken mostly through the entire being, in deep silence and is sometimes initiated by the exchange of a look, the touch of the fingers or the joining of hands, though this is by no means important.

My language is not a written or spoken one. It emanates from the heart and has no alphabet. And, yes, it has no question marks in its lexicon. Numerals are entirely missing, and, along with them, their brothers, the pluses, minuses, multiplications and divisions of mundane commerce.

My language may appear magical. Everything rhymes in it and yet poetry is but a pale shadow, the best song not much better. One does not speak it with sound, not hear it with the ears. One 'lives' it.

Needing no words, my language is seamless and timeless. And, one more thing, passing strange – this language cannot be learnt. We are born knowing it and remain knowing it all the while. However, only a very few are aware of my language because the routine sentences of ordinary speech which we are taught from childhood onwards hide it. Only those can use it who are able to forget what they've been taught – that languages need words, sentences, speech, grammar, cleverness.

It is not easy to do so. We 'know' that it is not possible to speak without words. In our knowledge lies our ignorance. Beyond this, where there is nothing else, beyond knowledge and ignorance, lies this eternal language, waiting patiently for us to realize its existence within ourselves.

My language has no vocabulary – for example, we cannot just speak of 'love' in my language. To do so would be like a person in a river, full and pure, talking about a spoon of water. So, I will not say my language is the language of love, compassion, belonging – these are just words and a poor substitute for what the language really conveys. My language has to be used to be known in all its depth and its uniqueness. The whole being speaks in this language to the whole universe.

When my language is spoken by a Master, the birds and trees, the fish and streams, the animals and forests, the wind and rain, all understand it before most people do, for they are what they are and their Self is not insulated by the veneer of mental gymnastics, which sometimes passes for scholarship, and often, for other things less noble.

I say all this as one who has 'heard' this language often and 'spoken' it, though not often enough. I have been fortunate in the grace of my Master and in the forgetfulness of my mind.

I would like to tell other disciples to stop looking for a mythical heaven and listen to my language. I want them to realize that a heaven does exist and that they are the rightful owners of it. However, the password which opens the gates of this heaven is in this language of the Masters, the silent language without words. Find a Master and experience it for yourself. You and your world will never be the same again.

# The Sound of No Hand Clapping

Many of us have heard the phrase, 'What is the sound of one hand clapping?' This is a famous koan of Zen master Hakuin Ekaku. It is an interesting koan to meditate upon. However, I would like to give you another one which is even more intriguing. It is this:

What is the 'sound' of no hand clapping?

Yes, this silent 'sound' exists, and it exists all the time in all of us. This is divine applause, and it needs no hands. It echoes in your heart. You cannot usually hear it because so many other sounds intrude.

And what is the applause for? It is for 'being'. Just being. Not being 'this' or 'that' with some label or the other attached to you. It is being 'this' or 'that' that creates the noise overwhelming the applause. It is labels that create expectations resulting in strengthening the hold of the ego.

Remember, it is the ego that has appointed itself the disc jockey for 'this' and 'that'. It plays its own songs at its own pace and the labelled you dances to these.

The divine in you—nay, the divine that you are—watches silently, laughing all the while. In moments when the mind is still and the music and dance stop, you can sense this silent laughter bubbling up from the centre of your being, unbidden and wonderful. For many of us, this feeling comes and goes, but it leaves a sense of well-being beyond the ordinary.

This bubbling laughter and the sense of bliss is the silent 'sound' of no hand clapping. It is the applause that emanates from YOU. Enlightened masters hear this all the time and you can see the evidence in the blissful calm in them and around them.

You and I, we can only hope and try. But remember, this is a counter-intuitive quest. You are not looking for something lost, for it is already there. Furthermore, actively seeking it and striving for it will keep it away from your reach forever. This is because all such striving is through the mind and it is the mind itself that overshadows the Real. The harder you 'think' about the goal, the stronger your mind becomes and the further the goal recedes. This is a strange quest indeed that involves losing more than finding.

The only way to achieve this bliss is by calming the mind. There are a few ways to achieve this. Self-enquiry is the most direct path. If you are interested, listen to the teachings of Ramana Maharshi, Papa ji, Swami Dayananda Saraswati and many other realized Masters like them, and internalize what they advise.

Before ending, I would like to give you a glimpse of the blissful world that these Masters live in. I must warn that I am only an occasional visitor and a novice to boot. I also write from memory of experiences past. Thus, my knowledge may be deficient in some respects.

In our day to day 'normal' world, where the ego rules, the road is strewn with emotional boulders. There are occasional potholes where anxiety is waiting for the unwary, as are anger, envy, greed and other such emotions. The past tries to colour the present, and the future beckons. Hope elates and fear depresses. Vanity often shapes the mood. 'Others' are separate and empathy is low. Boundaries are clear. Here 'Aham Brahmasmi' and 'Shivoham' are just words to be repeated by rote and you have as much chance of discovering your inner Brahma or Shiva by chanting these by rote, as you have a chance of soaring into the sky by chanting Jatayu-asmi a million times.

I have found that none of this happens in this other wonderful world. The road is clear and smooth. The past does not occupy our thoughts, and the future does not hold sway. All that is, is NOW. One moves here on a given path like the earth moves around the sun, without conscious thought. No morality is here, just a sense of 'rightness'. Emotional distortions and diversions are entirely absent. One finds an empathic echo in all creation, including people, animals, birds, trees and even rocks. Boundaries vanish and there are no 'others'. The sense of calm is all pervading. All is as it should be.

Here I can say Aham Brahmasmi and feel one with Brahma. Or I can say Shivoham and be Shiva. However, it never strikes me to repeat these words in this place. I have no need for these labels or phrases. Here, like Mansoor al Hallaj, 'ana al haq'! I am the Truth. What more can one want?

I would love to stay here forever but the ego insistently nudges me back into the humdrum world.

The fruit is ripening and, as Nisargadutta Maharaj said, one day it will fall, never to go back. It is enough to know that it will happen, sooner or later. Till then occasional experiences of the no hand clapping will have to suffice.

# My Life & Me

I have resolved so many times to seduce life so that it does my bidding. Instead, every time life has seduced me. It has made me turn away from my heart and do what it wants done through my mind.

I have resolved so many times to listen to my soul but in terming it 'mine' I have alienated it and made it the 'other'. It has repeatedly tried to make me aware that I am a part of it, and it is not the other way around. I ignore its soft voice and keep riding my ego to my destiny. The ego does not know my true nature, has no idea of what I came here to do, and does not know how to do it. Yet, it rules my life and, together, we keep wandering aimlessly here and there.

I have resolved so many times to dwell in silence. Yet, my life is very noisy. It talks incessantly and often sings its songs full of emotion. Its voice is sometimes disturbing, often alluring. I keep busy listening to what it is saying, when I know fully well that salvation lies in the gaps between the words and in the blank margins on either side. These words, however, do ego's bidding and keep me involved in their mesh.

My language has failed me, my gestures are those of a puppet, controlled by the ego and my thoughts a mish-mash of the humdrum. All the while, like a wonderful raga in the background, I remain aware of 'my' soul. Sometimes, in a mind cluttered by ego's detritus, I find a rare silent corner now and then and sway to this sublime melody. At such times only I am there, both the listener and the singer, and all is as it was meant to be. Sadly, such interludes are few and far between.

One day, I promise my ego will answer to me and I will no longer be a slave to its vagaries. One day I will gather the courage to look beyond the obvious and become one with the true 'ME' in 'me'. Then, and then alone can my silence shatter complacency and my stillness move mountains.

# An Eagle Told Me This

Once, when I flew with eagles high, one said to me with a sigh, "You humans are such misguided creatures. You must have some awful teachers." I'm a soaring eagle, sharp of eye. When I smelled smoke, even this high, I looked down from the sky. Nests were burning, I asked why, and I got this reply:

"We worship the Ice god, they worship Snow, and we often let them know, they must do as we said. They did not and they're dead! We burnt their homes, sent them to hell. We did our god's bidding well. These blasphemers with a false god, fully deserved what they got!"

I can't understand them at all. For all us birds, large and small, Earth, Water, Wind and Sun, keep alive everyone. We feel the Wind god under our wings. We see the Sun and other things, but humans kill for an imagined god. We birds find it very odd!

We can't understand your hue and cry. We've never seen dead birds fly, to come and tell us after they die, about any god in their sky. We birds pray as we wish, and so does every animal and fish. Our Simurgh has taught us well, "Don't make up heaven or hell."

A bird who says she won't pray, is free to do as she may. If another says, "I dislike the Sun", he flies at night for food and fun. Humans go to lands afar, to burn nests for causes bizarre, while Earth, Sun, Wind and Water, wonder at their wanton slaughter!

Down there, I see you feuding men, and I can't even remember when you didn't kill like fiendish fools, as per your own made-up rules. These men feel that they must, turn countless smiles to dust in their unchecked fanatic lust, to prove only 'their' god is just!

It's sad, as sad can be, to fly over land and sea, and watch your savagery time and again, your gleeful infliction of pain. In the name of god who you say is kind, in the name of god you can't find, while you're alive here and now, but you believe in, anyhow.

If it was indeed true, that a merciful god cared for you, he'd have killed these murderers all, and made the mildest stand tall. But that hasn't happened, we well know. These evil ones flourish and grow. Your meekest just sigh and sigh, hoping for better, when they die.

And though none has returned after dying, they keep on blindly trying, for a heaven promised after life, by those causing all this strife. No one has seen this heaven at all, or a hell for those who 'fall', but some use these clever lures, to keep the gullible, within their doors.

I said earlier and say again, your elders have twisted your brain. You humans are such misguided creatures. You must have some awful teachers. Away from your violence that I see, I stay in the sky, flying free, with our living gods, who I tell, "Please keep us birds and animals well!"

The eagle added, as I turned to leave, "I'll tell you something you must believe, and tell humans in every quarter—**Snow and Ice are both Water!**"

❧

I've thought often about what the eagle said
What if we'd been like them instead
And never hated people for how they prayed
What a difference that would've made!

❧

# What I Saw at the Conference of the Birds

## *In search of Simurgh*

Sometimes, in certain states of being, time does not exist for the likes of us. The past, present and future all are ours to explore. In one such felicitous period, I heard from Farid ud-Din Attar that there was to be a conference of birds with the intent of discovering the wondrous bird, Simurgh, the epitome of enlightenment.

Earlier I had travelled with Zarathustra on his quest, which was similar to this one, and at a number of turns found that he had a shallower understanding of the phenomenon of enlightenment than he thought he had. I was thus interested in seeing what the conference of the birds was trying.

When I reached the venue in Persia, about nine centuries back in human terms, I was not quite surprised to find that some others also had the same idea. After all, we are birds of a feather in more than one sense.

There was the Bennu bird from Egypt, a cousin of mine who broke the primordial silence when he flew over the surface of chaos and let out a cry. I also saw there, Anzu from Sumeria, with the body of an eagle and the head of a lion. He had told me the interesting story of how he stole the Tablet of Destinies, which gave him the powers of the gods and power over the mortal world. I saw the shape-shifting Boobrie from Scotland smiling at me. She had decided to take the form of an angel for this gathering. The majestic Garuda from India was there too, so brilliant in his colours that one could mistake him for the god of fire. Once he had confided in me that when he visited Japan, he was called Karura.

Then, I saw the Alkanost from Russia, whose songs were so enchanting that they made one forget every other desire. The Caladrius from Rome was also there. He had once used his powers to cure a relative of mine as he could absorb disease and then fly away with it, curing himself as well.

I met Fenghuang, my Chinese cousin, who had flown all the way to Persia to watch the conference of birds. Like most of us, he/she is immortal. His/Her appearance here was a good omen, as it foretold of harmony. Though no emperors were ascending the throne here, the chosen birds were embarking on a journey far more momentous than a mere coronation.

Then there was the Hoopoe, with her powers of healing and water divination, very useful skills in its native Arabia. She was the leader of this conclave, standing head and shoulders above other birds in her wisdom.

Of all those present there, only the Hoopoe could see us. She smiled at me and I bowed to her. Though an old friend, she is the alter ego of an enlightened master and deserving of respect. After all, she had once saved King Solomon when he was stranded in the desert.

We sat around this assembly of birds watching the Hoopoe greet all those who had come. I saw the Wagtail, the Parrot, the Partridge, the Falcon, the Quail, the Nightingale, the Peacock, the Pheasant, the Turtle-dove, the Pigeon, the Hawk, the Goldfinch, and many others, too.

The Hoopoe then addressed the assembled birds. When she said, "I am a messenger of the world invisible," she glanced at me with a knowing smile. I smiled back.

She then proceeded to speak to the birds to find out who would be willing and able to travel in search of the Simurgh. After hearing the Nightingale, she said, "O Nightingale, you who would stay behind dazzled by the exterior form of things, cease to delight in an attachment so deluding." She listened to the Parrot and told him, "O you, who have no idea of felicity! He who is not willing to renounce his life is no man."

And so it went with the Duck, who loved water too much, the Partridge, with its fondness for precious stones, the Hawk, with his attachment to outward forms of things, the Heron, with his love for the sea, and the Owl, with his love of riches and the hypocritical Sparrow.

The boastful Humay was there, too, though not a bird. After listening to him, the Hoopoe told him, "O slave of pride! Spread no more your shadow and boast no more of yourself. At this moment, far from conferring power upon kings you are like a dog busy with a bone."

When the birds expressed doubts about leaving their tranquil lives and finding Simurgh, Hoopoe told them about the essence of the quest. She said, "He who loves does not think about his own life; to love truly a man must forget about himself, be he ascetic or libertine. If your desires do not accord with your spirit, sacrifice them, and you will come to the end of your journey. If the body of desire obstructs the way, reject it; then fix your eyes in front and contemplate. An ignorant person will ask, "What connection is there between belief or unbelief, and love?" But I say, "Do lovers regard their lives? The lover sets fire to all hope of harvest, he puts the blade to his neck, he pierces his body. With love comes sorrow and the heart's blood. Love loves the difficult things."

Despite the Hoopoe's warning most of the birds wanted to go on the quest and we finally embarked upon this journey with thousands of them. Many stories were told on the way, most of them very elevating for those who could understand.

I will not recount the journey itself, which took us over seven valleys, because the journey for all those seeking the Simurgh for themselves is unique. What worked for the thirty birds who succeeded will not work for you, for you are not them. Let me summarise, though.

The seven valleys were valleys of love, understanding, independence, detachment, unity, astonishment, and finally poverty and nothingness.

In the quest we watched the birds undergo many difficulties and trials. Once all these tests were successfully passed, we moved to the valley of Love with those birds who did not fall by the wayside for one reason or another. There we learnt that love has nothing to do with reason. Then on to the valley of Understanding, where the remaining birds realized that knowledge is temporary, but understanding endures. When we overcome faults and weaknesses it brings us closer to the goal.

After this came the valley of Independence and Detachment. All desire to possess anything or any wish to discover faded away here. The birds had to renounce inner and outer attachments so that they could become self-sufficient.

In the valley of Unity, the Hoopoe told the birds that although they may see many beings, in reality there is only One, which is complete in its unity. As long as duality remains, good and evil will arise; but when they lose themselves in the divine essence, they will be transcended by love.

In the valley of Deprivation and Death, the Hoopoe informed the birds that they will realize that the individual self does not really exist. Eventually, the drop becomes part of the great ocean, forever in peace.

This was a difficult quest. Most of the thousands of birds who had started the journey had collapsed on the way. Some died of hunger or weakness. Predators took some others. The cold and the difficulty of the journey ended the lives of many. I could count only thirty birds among those who could go through the final valley.

Though I knew how it would end, seeing realization dawn on someone is something I can watch again and again. It is a blissful moment, the combination of awe and wonder, of unbeckoned laughter, too.

When these thirty reached the final stage, this is what happened.

When they were completely at peace and detached from all things they became aware that the Simurgh was there with them, and a new life began for them. All that they had done previously was washed away.

To their bewilderment and amazement, these thirty birds could see the Simurgh in the reflection of each other's faces. At last, in a state of contemplation, they realized that they and the Simurgh were one and the same being.

This was the moment I was waiting for. The wonder, the inner laughter, the sheer sense of bliss was all there, as it was for me and for countless others who have successfully undergone this quest.

This reminded me of the story the Garuda had once told me. When the gods and demons were fighting to get divinity for themselves, the gods went to Brahma and requested him to hide it where no one could get it. Brahma thought and rejected the sea, land and sky as appropriate hiding places, since these were accessible to someone or the other. He finally hid divinity inside men and women, for he said, no one will ever think of looking for it there.

Some do, though, and after a strenuous quest, even find it. They then discover that the destination is truly worth the journey.

Who am I, you may ask. Well, I am the Phoenix. I live through many births and once every five hundred years or so, when I feel the time is right, I end my life in a burst of fire, only to rise from the ashes again. Fortunately, my learning and wisdom remain with me through this fiery transition.

Why, you may wonder, do I subject myself to combustion? I just take Fariduddin's advice literally – "If you wish to find the ocean of your soul, then die to all your old life and then keep silent!"

If you want further elaboration, I can only recount the story of the moths that I heard on the journey through the seven valleys.

When moths desire to unite with the flame of a lamp, some are scared of the heat when they get near the lamp and fly away. They get nowhere. Only the moth that enters the flame and annihilates itself, gets what it desires. As the wise moth said when he saw that the flame and the moth appeared to be one, "He has learnt what he wished to know; but only he understands, and one can say no more."

Maybe, one day, you, too, will want to understand.

# When the Mirror Breaks

## *Thoughts on the Nature of Reality*

I keep my toothbrush in a glass. This glass is kept in front of the large mirror on my bathroom wall. One morning, I had an early meeting and, in a hurry, I tried grabbing the mirror image of my toothbrush.

Suddenly it struck me that this was a metaphor for our existence. I felt that this metaphor was at three levels. Each of these levels is linked to the next, however tenuously.

At the first level is how we perceive reality. We assume that the reality we perceive is a true representation of how things are. However, it is merely a mirror image mediated by the nature of our perception. A bird would perceive the same reality differently. Through a microscope, it would be entirely different. The same goes for thoughts, too. The 'mirror' in this case is made of our senses and our mindset.

At the second level, we ourselves—our body-mind—are the image in the mirror whereas reality, whatever that is, exists on the other side. What comprises the 'mirror' in this case? It is our belief that we are merely the body-mind. In our body consciousness we have posited a universe where three-dimensional space-time rules. We see and sense objects through our facilities. Using our instruments, and mathematics, we try to make sense of what we sense. At this level, we are still subject to the laws of space-time as they exist for us.

The third level is somewhat more abstruse. It is one step beyond the second level. In this, the 'mirror' breaks. All space becomes us and, if we are to go by the experience of those who have attained this state, time ceases to exist, at least in the way we are used to perceiving it. Our normal senses are also overshadowed by other 'senses', which are far more perceptive. Mundane physical laws, discovered till now, do not constrain our existence.

This is scientifically counter-intuitive but we need to keep in mind two important things – firstly, our science belongs to the second level and, secondly, phenomena which appeared magical in the not-so-distant past, have been explained by science, and science has gone even beyond that predicting and proving things we could not even observe. Keeping this in mind, it is not beyond the realm of possibility that science will one day catch up with what happens when the mirror breaks.

Where am I in this scheme of things, at the present time? I am edging closer to the mirror, coming to terms with its existence and trying to learn how to break it. Not an easy thing to do, considering that it is said to be an explosive event, born of absolute calm.

# Ramadhan

Let the night not turn into day, and fasting become feasting, just after you pray. Listen all who have gone without food and water – you have done it because you are pious. Do not forget this piety when the daylight fades. The blessings of the crescent moon fall not on those whose hearts are empty and stomachs full.

Waste not the bounty of God. Each grain of rice you take has your name written on it and those that are thrown away are counted by Him who knows all. Those that you eat in excess of your need are counted amongst these, too. From these he subtracts those you give to the less fortunate.

Work is worship. How can you think that you will gain merit by shirking work? Yes, you fast, but His messenger fasted too, and worked all the more. Think of those for whom this fasting is year long, for they have naught to eat. Think of them and thank Him for His blessings showered on you. Deserve these by working towards the betterment of His world, of which He has made you a temporary custodian. Is your repayment going to be laziness?

God is compassionate and merciful. Reflect this in your small way in everything you do. Anger has no place in His kingdom. Remember this, when unaccustomed hunger makes you irritable. Think of Him who watches, yes, even your unspoken thoughts. Think of Him and marvel at your good fortune. Be deserving of it, calm and peaceful in your thought and deed and merciful towards all His creatures. One word spoken in anger, even a dark thought in the depths of your mind, is like a cake eaten during the fast.

Fasting is not only of the stomach. It is of the ego, too. Let your ego not reign unchecked because you have possessions aplenty. In His eyes, these are like nothing. You stand before Him naked in body and mind, for He knows all. Humility is the manna you survive on. If you abandon it, then you might as well sin in other ways, too. At least you will have passing pleasure before all is taken away on judgement day, forever.

Judge not others and do not have others judge you. There is only He who can judge; yes, He who knows all. If you harbour negative thoughts, He sees you in the shadow of these. Those who are innocent bask in His light, and no shade darkens their shapes. Be of them, kind and understanding. In His kingdom you will need these qualities. Practice them now, so you are not found wanting.

Sound was given unto you, to enable you to survive in this world. He sees how you make use of this gift. He has no need of sound, and sits in silence within you, giving you sustenance and keeping you alive. In the silence of the mind His hymns can be heard in the core of your heart, and the pathway to Him remains clear. Silence, indeed is golden.

Thoughts are silent sound. They smile, they laugh, they scold. They beckon and they repulse. Watch your thoughts, for He watches them too. Why fast with your face if you keep feasting with your mind? You may fool yourself and others around you, but He sees all and knows you for what you are.

Be cheerful. He does not like sombre faces or he would not have given the ability to smile and laugh. Look at infants, those closest to Him. Do they not gurgle and laugh as if they still see Him waving to them? If he wanted His chosen ones to be sober and severe, infants would have had thunderous brows and frowning mouths, for they are the dearest to Him. Yes, He gave tears, too, but keep them in reserve to wash away the grains of sand which fate sometimes puts in your eye.

Spread joy wherever you go. Let whatever you touch be better for your having touched it. He expects no less.

And though the fasting may cease till next year, the heart should remember to be kind and the mind remember to be wise all the year around. Let the resolve to work hard persevere. Those who slacken their goodness just because the fast has ended, do themselves no favours. Remember, He who sees all, sees all not only during one month of the year. He is always there, smiling at you, ready with His gifts, if you are ready to receive them. Be always worthy of Him.

May the Holy Month end with all its blessings being showered on you.

# Meditations on the Four Sounds of Life

## *Para, Pashyanti, Madhyama, Vaikhari—and Fana and Baqa, Too*

Beloved,

We are not new in this world, you and I. Not as old as *Para,* from which we were born into *Pashyanti,* but we are certainly older than *Madhyama. Vaikhari* is merely our earthly avatar.

Going back, inwards, I get a glimpse of Para, our past and our ultimate future. I am sometimes one with you in Pashyanti. I often dream of you in Madhyama and, of course, consummate our marriage in Vaikhari, the expression of our hormonal desires.

These four, beloved, are the four forms of 'sound', explained by our seers. I understood them when I realized the difference between sound and noise. Noise is the audible sound born of vibration, whereas 'sound' in this context stands for the whole spectrum of consciousness, with Para at the transcendental end where thought originates, and Vaikhari at the earthy one. Pashyanti and Madhyama are shades in between, each seamlessly evolving into the subtler one, as wisdom dawns, and our perceptive consciousness becomes increasingly refined.

Vaikhari, as you may have guessed, is the physical expression of our consciousness. Often confused with 'love', it is mediated by our hormonal urges. This, of course, is essential for the survival of our species. Sometimes, it can also be destructive.

Yes, I think of your physical form in Vaikhari, dwell on its charm and revel in my blessings. I used to dream of you in Vaikhari, too, but, over the years, in these dreams, both while asleep and awake, I have started using Madhyama. Not surprising, since this comes from my centre, my very heart. Indeed, my feeling for you deserves more, but I have still to evolve. I have gone past the 'a' of 'akshara' and am moving towards the 'kshara' and beyond, but the goal is still a while away.

In blessed moments, I touch my soul and yours and, unexpectedly, we communicate in Pashyanti. Closer than close, beyond the mental and the physical, it is almost a trance language, spiritual in its lexicon. In these moments, I can sense the 'kshara' and get a small inkling of the 'Aum' beyond it, encompassing all. This transcends thought and the normal concept of being. In these magic moments, I see no difference between you and me.

In Pashyanti, I am awake, yet not awake. I exist, yet this 'existence' is beyond mere living. I have a body, yet I am not aware of it. More surprisingly, you have a body, but I am not aware of that, either. Nor of your mind or mine. It is an all-encompassing being, one where what usually matters, doesn't matter. During these moments, I soar in a strange world where there are no others. I do not even feel love, only belonging. I can sense the unstruck sound, the Anahata nada, here.

The feeling passes and I return to the 'normal' world, with you in my arms. I am still very much in love, but I am alive in Vaikhari again.

I look back and often feel that there can be no state beyond Pashyanti. What more can be there when, along with you and I, all 'others' have ceased to be? Have I not experienced all that seers strive for, the state where I become one with the Universe? And then I laugh at my presumption.

My feeling is not surprising. After all, I am thinking in Vaikhari, the language of illusion.

I shake my head and try to relive what I could sense beyond the edge of Pashyanti. Para was there, waiting, beckoning. Para the ultimate transcendental sound beyond Jagrat, Svapna and Sushupti, the state which Indian seers have described as Turiya and Sufis as Baqa.

What I had experienced was merely a glance of Fana, the death before death, where Pashyanti is the lingua franca and from where one can and does come back. I had returned, entranced by where I had been and, to prove the fact of my return, entranced by you, close to me, yet, once more, 'another'.

One day, my love, we will be together in Pashyanti again and, as one, use it as a bridge to enter Para, the Aum beyond Akshara.

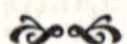

> PS: *Para is the first stage of 'sound' and is the origin of thought. It is intuitive and beyond sound and concepts. Pashyanti denotes our intellectual consciousness, an unspoken idea. In Madhyama there is a clear distinction between the sound and the object it denotes. Vaikhari, represents the physical consciousness or is an audible manifestation of speech.*
>
> *Saint Tyagaraja mentions that the Supreme consciousness or Nadabrahman manifests itself as Shabdabrahman through the power of Maya Shakti. It emerges first as Para Vani in the Mooladhara, then as Pashyanti in the Manipura, next as Madhyama in the Anahata and then eventually as Vaikhari in the Vishuddha.*

# My Anand & the Eunoia That I Experience

## *My journey's here and now*

Anand literally means bliss. It is one element of an ancient trilogy – *sat-chit-anand* (Sanskrit: सच्चिदानन्द) which includes sat (truth) and chit (consciousness). It is the real nature of ultimate reality – All-That-Is. Together the word satchitanand conveys a level of existence that only the truly enlightened can experience.

I am not one of these Masters. Far from it. I am still embroiled in day-to-day life mediated by my ego. However, I sometimes get glimpses of bliss, which anand refers to.

The practical manifestation of this is a sense of elation, without any specific cause. An undefinable laughter bubbling up in the chest, a 'wholeness' defining existence in the inner and outer milieu, devoid of any sharp edges.

Eunoia, the Greek word that Cicero translated as the Latin 'benevolentia', is what best describes this feeling. Conventionally, eunoia means kindness or benevolence towards others. In the context of my bliss, I sense it as a feeling of goodwill of the universe towards me.

Our lives are jigsaw puzzles comprising many diverse pieces. These pieces do not often fit together well. The shape of some pieces is wrong, sometimes the size is not correct, at other times one piece—most notably, the ego—tries to dominate all other pieces, occupying a disproportionate area in the puzzle pushing other softer puzzle pieces aside.

These pieces can change shape, colour and size as time passes. Whether they do this so that the whole is harmonious depends upon one's spiritual development. As one 'advances', the ego piece becomes smaller and smaller till it finds its apt place in the overall jigsaw, eventually just being there to ensure survival. Other pieces, too, lose their sharp edges. Many vanish altogether.

I find my own jigsaw puzzle coming together seamlessly, now and then, to spell B L I S S. In my case, this anand is a happy happenstance. When this happens, I feel the benignity of everyone and everything that I can see, their pure benevolentia towards me, untainted by anything mundane. I feel a similar eunoia going out of me, towards all. My universe tells me, then, that I belong to it and it belongs to me.

When under the spell of this blissful feeling, I cannot identify the individual pieces comprising the harmoniously completed jigsaw puzzle as separate elements. When the feeling passes, I look back at the puzzle pieces that came together for a short, blessed time. I find many different pieces small and big, each unique in shape.

There is a piece marked good health. Each good friend is there with his or her name on a different piece. Financial security is another important piece. A warm, welcoming place to stay that reflects my own ethos and that of my loved ones, is another piece. Each member of my family, close and not-so-close, is there as a separate piece, as are my work associates and the children who we are helping advance in life.

Many others have these same pieces in their own lives and yet most do not get this feeling of spontaneous bliss. I look more closely to see which special elements make all this come together as a harmonious whole.

My partner in life, my wife and best friend, is one such unique element. My meditation and the learning gleaned from our ancient texts, particularly the Upanishads and the Gita is another element. My affinity with, and the felt closeness to, Gurus such as Sai Baba of Shirdi, Ramana

Maharshi and Nisargadutta Maharaj, is an important force joining the other pieces together. Reading certain esoteric texts has also imparted their wisdom. The words of Sufis such as Mansour al Hallaj, Rumi and Farid ud-Din Attar have played a role, too. Realizing that all these wise ones, including Zen masters, spoke of the same reality reinforces my conviction that I am on the right path.

Then there is Rabiya al Adawiyya of Basra, who said,

*I carry a torch in one hand*
*And a bucket of water in the other*
*With these things, I am going to set fire to Heaven*
*And put out the flames of Hell*
*So that voyagers to God can rip the veils*
*And see the real goal*

When I could understand exactly what she means by this, and could internalize what our ancient texts and my Gurus and others taught, I saw the reality of heaven and hell and the entrapments of conventional religion. This wisdom led me to a glimpse of the real goal, which is the realization of the divine in myself. I knew then that making 'Aham Brahmasmi' or 'Shivoham' procedural, rather than merely declarative, is the objective.

I feel that all my learning from these wise teachers has helped nudge me towards this sublime goal by paring my ego down to size, so that it can fit in well with the other pieces. My anand is a consequence of this. In quiet, introspective moments, I take another look at the pieces coming together to make my spirit soar at times. I want to examine why this feeling comes and goes and is not permanent. I re-read what I have said above from the beginning, and found the answer right there. It made me laugh out aloud when I read the para mentioning 'there is a piece called good health'. I go on to identify my jigsaw puzzle pieces in worldly terms – financial security, friends and so on.

Real, permanent bliss does not depend upon the coming together of these kinds of pieces. I realized then that this mundane puzzle is merely a preliminary step. Even though it can help bring inner tranquility that a novice like me needs to experience fleeting bliss, it is still driven by the mind. I remember the enlightenment poem of the thirteenth century Japanese Zen mistress, the Abbess Adachi Chiyone, also known as Mugai Nyodai.

*With this and that*
*I tried to keep the bucket together,*
*and then the bottom fell out.*
*Where water does not collect,*
*the moon does not dwell.*

The bottom has to fall out and only when that happens there can be permanent bliss. Till the bottom falls out, my anand will not become permanent and will merely remain a happy happenstance.

I am still collecting this and that and the bottom is firmly still affixed in my bucket. The mind still rules, and it keeps me preoccupied with mundane things. My heart knows better and, once, under its influence, I wrote the following:

### At Heaven's Door

*I visited God last night, or his closed door, to be precise. On it was written, in letters bold, Entry barred, to Mind or Gold. Alas, my mind was with me on its high horse, full of knowledge, richly adorned and I had to turn back unfulfilled.*

*But my heart caught a glimpse of the Beloved and on the way back it whispered, "There was no door... "*

I know this now in theory. In practice, I have not started listening to my heart as much as is required. The password through the no-door is silence and my mind still makes too much noise. The following lines would reflect my situation better.

### The Here And Now

*Passions stilled*
*Emotionless, without desire*
*I sit*
*In the centre of incandescence*
*But life beckons*
*For time is not now*
*I leave reluctantly one womb for another*
*Which I had left as unwillingly before*

For now, the occasional glimpse of anand that I get will have to help in keeping the goal in mind. I will wait patiently for the time when I am ready, and the feeling of bliss becomes permanent.

I have reason to hope. As Nisargadutta Maharaj said, the fruit ripens slowly but falls suddenly, without return. I will then know what sat-chit-anand really means and will be able to proclaim with conviction like Mansour al Hallaj—"Ana al Haq!"—I am the Truth.

# Reflections On the Nature of Being

Tonight, before sleeping, I will meditate on the nature of consciousness. 'I am not my body' is not difficult to internalize. 'I am not my mind' takes more time, but I have come to terms with it after some practice. That leads me to think that I am my soul, my consciousness.

This, I realize, is wrong on two counts. The first mistake is in speaking in terms of 'my' soul. If the soul is 'mine', who is the 'I' who uses the possessive? No, the soul is not 'mine', I AM the soul.

The second mistake is in equating the soul with my consciousness.

Consciousness is a tool, a powerful yantra, of the Soul-I-Am, to be manipulated to create and mould my perceptual world. The Soul-I-Am is an independent entity possessing this consciousness.

Thus, it is obvious to me that I am more than my consciousness in the same way that the painter is more than his paints, or the poet is more than her pen. All my body-mind experiences are the paintings that I have created, and the poems I have written USING my consciousness.

It is also clear to me that the Soul-I-Am cannot merely be confined within my body. The body is in the Soul-I-Am and not the other way around. This very realization made something unexpectedly flip in the forefront of my brain. I find that this changes my perspective and, when I look in the mirror, I do not feel that what I see is all I am. Somewhat unsettling at first, it becomes normal soon.

I believe that the Soul-I-Am is of a higher level of magnificence of which, in this physical avatar, my mind can sense a very small part. In it exist all the lives I've experienced on this plane and perhaps on other planes as well, and, perhaps, all future lives I will experience. Other potentials belong to it as well – worlds my brain knows nothing about, creativity of an amazing order and understanding beyond the grasp of my limited mind. And it uses consciousness as a tool to actualize and experience whatever it wishes to experience.

I wonder why did the Soul-I-Am separate from the universal All-That-Is, and when, and I laugh at my presumption. I only have a wrench and I am trying to dismantle and understand a mystery that has no nuts and bolts. My physical brain has built-in limitations, and I will only understand some secrets when I have the ability to move beyond it, and directly use consciousness, the tool used by the soul.

Yes, this relationship between the soul and consciousness is fascinating and, tonight I'll meditate upon it before I sleep. Perchance my dreams will show the way and once this is settled, I will meditate upon whether I, as the Soul-I-Am, can be confined within this plane of existence, mediated by my bodily senses, and their limited view of the world as processed by my brain. If all this physical equipment that passes for my body-mind is inside the Soul-I-Am, obviously what I am is larger than my body-mind. My physical self sees the world around me within a very narrow spectrum and interprets it within its limitations. There is no logical reason, then, for the Soul-I-Am, with its own unlimited awareness, to be confined to the space-time and worldview which is projected by my physical self.

Yes, I'll meditate upon the different dimensions in which I may 'really' exist, beyond the obvious three spatial ones and Time. I look forward to this, with anticipation.

And, talking of Time, it strikes me that this is a rare kettle of fish by itself. Perhaps its secrets will astonish me, as so many other experiences have done – experiences which I could not have imagined before I embarked on this path. However, it is early yet. I will meditate on Time when the time is right.

# The Highway of Spirituality

## *The Roads of Religions*

Imagine an enchanted elevated highway between birth and death. It is a freeway, with no toll booths. No horns are permitted on this highway. Silence reigns, outer and inner. Traffic marshals are available in the form of guides, mostly on the ramps going up to this highway. Once the traveller is on the highway proper, the guides watch silently and come and advise at points where such advice is requested. They never intrude or try to impose their own rules.

Under this elevated highway there are many service roads. Some of these run parallel to the highway, below it, from the beginning to the end and have branches going out. There are ramps leading on to the elevated highway from these and other ramps leading down from the highway to these service roads. There are traffic lights and road signs aplenty. Rules and regulations abound and are drummed into the travellers. There are colourful digressions on these roads especially tailored to pamper the senses. Further away a branch leads you, the more digressions you encounter. These digressions, with their gaudy lights, can be seen from the highway and many an unfortunate traveller, who has reached there, is attracted enough by them to take the next exit down.

These service roads have guides on the way and many shops selling maps or, where there is but one map, many interpretations to guide the innocent and the not so innocent. Each road has people encouraging others to enter it, touting the greatness of their roads. They promise that their road is the best one to lead the traveller to a promised heaven. The competition to bring more and more travellers on one's road is often intense. Those preaching in favour of their roads are very passionate. Violence against those choosing other roads is not unknown.

Each road is noisy and tries to inveigle the senses using its colour and vivacity. There are places on these roads where the traveller may go for nourishment. There are places where sacrifices of one sort or the other may be offered. There are byways and spurs leading to places, sometimes ennobling, at others, dark and depressing. Some byways cause emotions of anger, some cause compassion. Some roads close to the highway have symbols and guides pointing towards the up-ramps. These symbols are often misunderstood, and people start worshipping them instead of going where they point. As we move away from the roads near the highway, we encounter more and more ritualistic behaviour and pandering to the senses.

These are not ordinary roads and the highway is not an ordinary highway. It hides secrets aplenty. Let me tell you five of these.

The first secret is this. Regardless of which road you choose to travel, one part of you, that which is beyond sacred, is always on the highway, urging you to take the next ramp up. Even if you choose not to take the ramp up, it speaks to you of the need to keep in the lane under the shadow of the highway which is the quietest and smoothest way forward, without digressions of one sort or the other and with the least interference from those intent on selling the virtues of a particular path. In the nature of things, its voice is gentle and often not heard in the loud noises of these roads.

Those who do hear and follow can be easily differentiated from those who do not, by their peaceful countenance, by the gentleness of their conduct and by their compassion. They can see and empathize with other people who are in a similar state on other paths parallel to theirs. They do not feel any need to urge others to follow their own path because they have realized that all those similar to them—those who are in touch with their personal guide on the highway—are moving with them towards a common goal, regardless of the path they follow. They also realize that others who have chosen to ignore this guidance will remain by the wayside, shouting the attractions of their paths, trying to lure the unwary by promising things which merely exist in their own imagination.

The second secret is that on this elevated highway, there are no rites and rituals. There are no places where sacrifices can be offered. God is only the appointed traffic policeman on the roads below and is not needed on the highway above.

The third secret is that this elevated highway has crossings which confer 'other-worldly' powers on the traveller. However, using these powers for one's own good or for ego satisfaction, leads the traveller to an 'exit only' ramp, which takes him or her out to one of the side-roads far away from the elevated highway.

The next secret is that counter-intuitive things can be expected on this elevated highway. There is no reverence here, no sense of holiness. There are no men or women, no kin or non-kin. Every traveller is unique and yet universal. This is a place of purity but it is not a sterile place. It has beauty and bliss and serenity beyond measure. Many conventional emotions such as anger, envy, lust, greed, etc. generally fall away as we move up the ramp. What was love for individuals becomes belonging. Joy is there but of an order not encountered below.

And now, the final secret – *the elevated highway continues beyond death.* The service roads end with death and, then, begin again with the next birth. The part of ourself which is always on the highway marks the place on the road where we ended our journey this time around and, in the next life, starts the traveller where he or she was at the end of this life.

It is up to each of us to decide which road to take, whether to climb up the ramp of this elevated highway and, if so, when. It is not a decision which is made easily. All baggage, including most conventional relationships and attachments, has to be left on the ramps going up on this highway. Most of us are very attached to what we have achieved, won and loved. We like the noises, sensations and tastes of the roadside, and it is difficult to leave these. I know, for I have been waiting half way up a ramp for some time, revelling in my surroundings, thinking about the next step forward. I can sense the wonders that I will encounter on the highway but am still attached to so many things needed to be left behind. Patience and faith are recommended by the guides. I am waiting patiently with absolute faith in my guide and, more importantly, in myself. I am certain these will help propel me above, to the highway, when the time it right.

# Is Our Glass Half Full?

Our glass is almost always half full. For some, it is half full of love and laughter, for others it contains humdrum things. For an unfortunate few, it is filled with angst or bile.

Regardless of what our glass is half full of, we overlook one very crucial reality.

We usually ignore the other half of the glass. It is not really empty, unless, of course, we are in outer space. Here, on earth, it contains air. We need not choose to live in the bottom half of the glass. We can live in the half that contains air. However, most of us believe that we do not have this choice, and that we must live in the half of the glass that is full. While this is great for those whose glass is half full of good things, it is really dismaying for those whose glass is half full of humdrum things and for those whose glass contains angst or bile.

This misunderstanding cannot be emphasized strongly enough. It makes the lives of those whose glass contains only humdrum things, pedestrian and boring. Theirs is a grey existence in a colourful world.

For those, whose glass is half full of negative things, this misunderstanding is even worse. It makes the world a much darker place than it needs to be, not only for them but also for those around them. We must realize that we do not have to live with the angst in our lives or with the consequent bile. We can live above it. If we strongly believe this, then the negativity can only touch us if we let it do so.

If we choose not to let the negativity in the bottom half of the glass affect us, we usually notice something strange. We find that the angst dissolves and changes into whatever we want it to, brightening our lives and those of others around us.

There are many reasons why more people don't try this, even though it sounds so easy.

Firstly, as mentioned earlier, most of us think that our place is at the bottom half of the glass. This makes us feel that our world is made up of the stuff surrounding us. If this stuff is dark, it is difficult to see the clear air above it, and we do not even try to get out. This leads to self-pity, blaming others, bemoaning our fate, futile anger and dark depression, making our surroundings even darker than they are. Good counselling, and a sincere desire to get out of one's present state is important in this case.

The second reason is that this stuff is sticky. Sometimes when we try to rise above this, the miasma follows us, and makes us think that we cannot escape it despite trying to. This makes us lose hope and we collapse into our previous state. A good teacher, loving family support and/or great friends who live in their clear spaces, are a great help in this situation.

Then there is reinforcement. The company we keep makes us see the world, not as it can be, but as it is for those around us. If we see negativity all around, we take this to be the world's natural state, and do not try for anything else. We become victims of confirmation bias. If this is the state of our current life, we must move ourselves to be amongst those who have a rosier outlook on life. Diversion, laughter, and firm refusal to take the negativity in one's life to heart, are important exits from this state.

The fourth is clinical depression. This case is different from the above. In this case, the weight of our mental health has made us submerge into an inner darkness. Our dark half-glass is formed of this. A psychological or medical intervention is required in this case. When treated well, the darkness in such lives can vapourize.

It is up to us to choose where we live. We should make this choice keeping in mind the advice of those far wiser than us.

The seventh and eighth of Solon's ten commandments are useful to remember. The seventh says *Make reason your supreme commander* and the next one is *Do not associate with people who do bad things*. This is advice truly worth heeding.

And, then, there is the fifth verse of Chapter VI of the Bhagawad Gita: *Let a man lift himself by his own Self. Let him not demean himself. The Self is the friend of the Self and the Self is the enemy of the Self.*

Let us introspect and strive to be our own friends and rise above to live in the upper half of the glass. This is the true habitat of our better nature, and dwelling here, we can make our world worthy of living in.

# You May Be Living In a Slum...

If I were to tell you that you are living in a shanty on the grounds of someone else's mansion and that your basic work is to count the landlord's treasure and clean, adorn and defend the mansion, you will reply that I am talking nonsense. If I then point out that, even more surprisingly, you live there voluntarily, and are not even paid for your effort, or rewarded by the landlord in any other way, you will definitely think that I must be drunk. Your reaction is understandable, but please bear with me. What I say is indeed true for almost all of us. It is just that we need to change our perspective and be more honest with ourselves.

Most of us are cognitive tenants living on the grounds of mansions owned by film celebrities, sports persons, leaders, political parties and religions. These are our landlords.

We spend our time counting the achievements of the objects of our 'admiration' – how many records they broke, how much money they earned, how many elections they won, new adherents they converted, etc. We try to polish up their flaws to put forth their best possible image on social and other media. We adorn them with our own praise for their achievements and we defend them vehemently against critics. We spend time scouring social media to identify and troll the latter. Often, our 'sentiments are hurt' if someone says something against our landlord. This hurt is particularly severe if our landlord happens to be Religion. Some may even stake their very lives in its defence.

We do all this voluntarily and the landlords do not pay us anything for our time and effort. They mostly ignore us but may, off and on, throw a bone in our direction through photo ops. With great pride we frame these photos. They show us grinning idiotically while the celebrity or leader looks on patronizingly.

We live on the properties of these landlords in groups of like-minded tenants who form our psychosocial slum cluster.

The tragedy is that most of us do not even realize that we are living in this cluster of shanties as unpaid serfs and wasting our time, instead of living in our own houses and improving them.

It is natural to wonder why we voluntarily become cognitive slaves of someone else, instead of living our lives as self-propelled, free-thinking individuals. There are many reasons for this.

Conditioning plays a major role in deciding which psychosocial slum cluster we join. This is especially true in case the mansion belongs to a religion. We are indoctrinated in the perceived greatness of the landlord in the mansion belonging to 'our' religion.

Often, we identify with the founder of our religion. We try to get as many 'outsiders' to come and reside in our cluster with us. We show animosity when they don't. Sometimes, this leads to violence against critics. There are constant cries of 'Our mansion is in danger' from some such clusters to motivate others living here to be on constant guard. Those who leave the premises to be free, or to join any other clusters, are not viewed kindly.

A similar behaviour pattern is observed when the landlord is a political party or leader.

Then there is transference. We love our country. A political leader shows that he does things for the country that we would love to do if we were in this leader's position. We transfer our love for our country to love for this leader, and join the psychosocial slum cluster on his grounds.

One other factor is 'experience taking'. This is what psychologists call our mindset when we subconsciously take on traits, attitudes and behaviour of our landlords. In extreme cases, we may replace our own persona with that of our landlords. Extreme religious identification with their deities by some advanced adherents is an example of this. Often, viewers start identifying with certain characters in a novel or in a movie. A whole field of psychology of fandom has examined this behaviour pattern.

One interesting experiment was done about how we let our own personality be overwhelmed by that of our landlord. Psychologists had people reading a story in front of a mirror. They found that, when they do this, subjects find it more difficult to identify with any character in the book because their own image in front of them is a constant reminder of their persona.

Confirmation bias strengthens the ties that bind us in our voluntary slavery. It confirms our adulation of our landlord and dulls our critical facilities vis-à-vis him or her. We live in our psychosocial slum cluster with other like-minded people, all of whom agree with our views about our landlord. This makes us stronger in our belief by assuring us that so many others can't be wrong. We are aware that there are many outside our mansion's grounds who are critical of our 'landlord', but, instead of introspecting, we become defensive and even more set in our views.

All this boils down to deep empathy with a person, place, faith, etc. This originates in a part of our brain, called the right supramarginal gyrus. This very small lobe of our brain plays a very large part in our lives indeed.

If we have to break free of our psychosocial slum clusters, we need to overcome the factors that pushed us into it, and keep us there. In order to do so, we must constantly stand in front of the mirror of our own ideas and reinforce the notion that we are free beings who can think for ourselves. We must then be willing and able to disagree with our fellow slum cluster dwellers. This will surprise them because the residents of these clusters do not like freedom of thought. They cannot understand critical balance and it challenges their set views.

Getting out of the psychosocial slum cluster is easier said than done but if we are truly sincere, we can start by being sceptical of all we see and hear, both about the positive qualities of our own landlord and the constant criticism of other landlords that we hear in our cluster. This applies to all landlords, but it applies particularly to those owning the mansions of politics or religion. We can then slowly ease our way out of the landlord's grounds. Of course, other residents may throw us out in confused anger quite quickly.

The alternative is to keep living in slavery on someone else's mansion grounds. We will then spend our entire life counting the landlord's treasure and cleaning, adorning and defending their mansion, instead of changing our own present and future for the better.

## On Spiritual Enlightenment

The essence of the teachings of Ramana Maharshi and Nisargadutta Maharaj and other realized masters hailing from different cultures, is in the following quotes:

**Ramana Maharshi:**

"The method is summed up in the words 'Be still'. If you reach the state where there is neither sleep nor movement of mind, stay still in that, the natural (real) state."

"When one remains without thinking one understands another by means of the universal language of silence."

**Nisargadutta Maharaj:**

"I am awareness, without being aware of awareness."

"When I am unity, then that is pure awareness which is not aware of its awareness, and there can be no subject and object – therefore there can be no witnessing. Any manifestation, any functioning, any witnessing, can only take place in duality."

"To expound and propagate concepts is simple, drop all concepts is difficult and rare."

This experience has been referred to by Japanese Buddhist masters as Satori. It means awakening, comprehension or understanding. The deep experience of seeing one's true nature is called kensho. Ken is 'seeing', and sho means 'nature' or 'essence'.

This is the experience that led Rabiya al Adawiyya to say, 'In your light I learn how to love, in your beauty, how to make poems. You dance inside my chest, where no one sees you! Ali Shah, Pir of Dewa Sharif also exclaimed – 'There is no space to go down in supplication. He is in me!'

## My Birthday Candles & Yours

There was one candle on my first birthday cake and there'll be one candle on my last. Through this journey from one candle to one candle, I'll live in a drama where sometimes I am a villain, sometimes a hero, often a main player but mostly an extra, watching events pass by in which I have no say.

It is a morality tale, this drama, with lessons in every act. No one shouts 'quiet' on the sets here, and there is plenty of noise. I feel sorrow and joy, disappointment and triumph, dismay and satisfaction, excitement and boredom, pain and ecstasy, and so many other things.

And none of it is real. Oh, it is real enough to make me cry or laugh, but these tears and laughter are felt by the celebrator of birthdays, the actor whose role I am playing this time around, not by one who will go home at the end of this episode.

Did I tell you that I have been born countless times? That I have died the same number of times, less one? No?

In truth, you see me at the mundane level only, but I am not this body, nor this mind. And, it may surprise you to know, neither are you. We are just actors here on this set, playing roles we decided ere we took birth. We voluntarily subjected ourselves to this emotion ridden existence in the physical world to learn things that are best learnt here. We had set our course true, but it was modified when our ego took the tiller. As of now, I am struggling with it to keep the bow pointed towards where I want to go, before I depart this plane.

Mourn not my passing, for the real actor does not die, though his body may lie in his coffin on the stage. There have been many coffins and many funeral pyres in which I was the centrepiece, and there will be many more, till I do not need to learn from these dramas any more.

All these roles that I have played on various stages in times past, live on in me at some level, sometimes appearing in my dreams, sometimes in my actions and often in my thoughts. There are men in here and women, too, at this point, perhaps in equal measure. We are collectively who I am.

All the while I keep thinking: Who is it beyond my physical self, beyond my body-mind? Who is the life in me, the user of the consciousness, guiding my senses? At a deeper level I know that only when I stop thinking, I will realize the truth of who I am, but this is not easy to do.

The mind is too strong and too protective of its existence and too wary of inner silence. It insists that these senses that I use are my only gateway to the world, but I know it lies. Or, perhaps, it does not know any better, and its awareness is confined to its realm. That I can consider possibilities beyond this realm, gives me hope.

These senses mediated by the mind belong to the actor whose role I am playing. The real me has super senses held at bay at this stage of my advancement by these physical ones. I can only access them if I completely silence my insistent mind.

Till that happens, the number of candles on my birthday cakes will keep changing, till they return to one, and then, beyond the role-play, none.

We will meet in the hereafter again, you and I. Then we will assess what we have learnt and what more is needed. We will perhaps script another drama together in this theatre and light more birthday candles for each other.

In the meantime, in the here and now, let's make the best of what we have on this stage, with as much harmony as we can muster.

# On Meditation

Haribhai was a regular at the temple. He was an intelligent and shrewd person, and the biggest shopkeeper in the village. He was the trader who handled the village produce, selling it in the nearby town-market. He was also a devout person and came to the temple once a week. One day, he discussed meditation with the Master.

H: Master, yesterday you told Jamuni Ma about trying to find herself. You said to keep thinking about who she is. Are you advising meditation?

M: Haribhai, if you must put a label on it, yes, we should meditate upon who we are.

H: My Guru had told me to meditate while concentrating upon a candle.

M: Perhaps at that stage in your spiritual development, your Guru felt that this was the best for you. However, we do not stay in the same class all the time and lessons learnt in the next class are different.

H: So, now I should not meditate while concentrating upon a candle?

M: You must realize that everything in the universe is one. Anything that reinforces duality does not make it easier to reach this realization. When you meditate while concentrating upon an object, you perceive that object external to yourself. This reinforces duality and is a barrier to your becoming one with the universe. That is why I do not advise you to concentrate on anything other than the Self.

H: So, we should concentrate on the Self.

M: Yes, keep asking yourself who you really are.

H: Some people say that we should keep our eyes on the third eye, between the eyebrows.

M: What do you mean? Can you show it to me?

Everyone started looking at Haribhai. He tried to bring his vision to the centre of the eyebrows and succeeded in looking comically cross-eyed. Everyone laughed out aloud, including the Master.

M: Is that how you want to look when you are trying to meditate?

H (smiling): No, not really.

M: This is the danger of taking everything very literally. Let me explain why this misunderstanding has arisen. There are two reasons. In a certain meditative stage, the attention focuses by itself at the top of the nose, between the eyes. However, it is an automatic thing, not a forced one. Then, again, beginners are usually asked to concentrate on their breathing, to bring order to their mind by establishing a rhythm, and by giving the mind something to focus on. Well, one place to feel the breath is the top of the nose, between the eyebrows. So, you are asked to keep your attention here. Unfortunately, some people take it literally and try to become cross-eyed.

H: Yes, I can see that.

M: You must remember, in your spiritual practice, there is no place for physical contortions or for any pain. The goal is of stilling the mind and melding with creation. How can you still the mind when at every moment it is thinking of the pain you are inflicting on it?

H: Yet you say that we are not the body or the mind, so it does not really matter.

M: Good point. Once you realize that you are not the body, and not the mind, it does not matter. Even then the body does feel, and you would not like to inflict pain on yourself or others unnecessarily. However, till such time that this realization dawns, inflicting pain on oneself in the guise of religious practice is very counter-productive.

H: Must we sit in the lotus position while meditating? I cannot sit in this position anymore.

M: You can meditate in any posture you feel comfortable.

Someone in the crowd asked, "Even lying down?"

M (Looking at the questioner): Yes, even lying down. However, there is the danger of falling asleep if you meditate lying down or reclining. You should be comfortable but not that comfortable! (laughs, and others join him, then he resumes.)

M: Traditionally we are advised to sit in a comfortable position with the spine erect. It keeps the attention focused and alert. As chairs were not used in ashrams in Vedic times, the most comfortable position to sit was in the half-lotus or the full lotus. I feel that for sitting to meditate, it is still the most comfortable position. However, when you have travelled the path a bit, you will realize that it does not matter what posture your body is in or even where you are. You may be walking and meditating at the same time.

H: One more question, Master. Where should we concentrate while meditating on the Self?

M: There is no need to concentrate anywhere specific. You will realize this after a while. However, in the beginning you may keep your attention on the spiritual heart or the spiritual centre. This was the way prescribed by Ramana Maharshi and by my Master, who was a direct disciple of the Maharshi. I, too, followed this till such time that I did not need it anymore.

H: Where is the spiritual heart?

M: To the right of the physical heart. It is at the point where you usually point to yourself with your right hand when saying 'this is me'.

H: Can I feel the spiritual heart in the body?

M: This is not a physical organ like the lungs or the liver. It is a powerful psychic centre, one of the chakras in your spiritual Self. However, with practice you can feel the spiritual heart, as you can feel the Muladhara and the Lotus chakras.

H: I have always wanted to do so!

M: Why? Do not get too involved in these phenomena. Physical and psychic phenomena are pointless. They are obstructions in the path of the true seeker. Just pass them by. You must remain focused on your goal. What is your goal, Haribhai?

Before Haribhai could answer, someone said in a stage whisper, "To make lots of money!" Everyone laughed, including Maha'ajji and Haribhai. Maha'ajji kept silent for a moment, and when everyone was quiet once more, he said:

M: Let us forget the worldly things for the moment. Let me rephrase my question, "What is your spiritual goal?"

H (thinks awhile): It is peace of mind.

M: Well said. Permanent peace of mind can only be obtained when you realize your true Self. Till then, peace will come and go, for it is a play of your thoughts. When you realize your true Self, you are no longer a slave of your mind.

H (nods):

M: And, as I said earlier, the most direct way to do this is constant enquiry into who you really are. Meditate on the Self, if that phrase is more to your liking.

One of the visitors asked, "I have heard that there are some sadhus who can go into a samadhi and stay in it for years! Is that a result of meditation also?"

M: In the beginning I used to feel a great sense of achievement when I could go into samadhi. I made my mind blank, and peace would descend upon me. It was a very satisfying feeling and gave me a lightness of being. I thought that this was what meditation was all about. Then I asked my Guru. He told me that this was a very common misconception. He said that he had been corrected in this by Ramana Maharshi himself, who was not in favour of conventional forms of trance-like samadhis.

He called this state '*manolaya*'. In this the mind is suspended and the body loses the sense of time. Ramana Maharshi always said that this was a waste of time. At the end of the samadhi, the seeker started out where he was when he went into this state. If he was thinking of eating a banana five months back, he would think of eating a banana when he came out of samadhi. So, what was gained?

V: When you explain it this way, I understand what you mean.

M: Yes, such samadhis are like pressing the pause button on a video. The video pauses and remains stopped for as long as we want. When we push the play button again, the video starts exactly where it had stopped. Nothing new has been recorded or erased. Just some time has elapsed.

V: But if such a state happens naturally, what should we do?

M: As you progress on your spiritual path, this state will come sooner or later. It is a milestone on the path. If you go round and round the milestone, you will stop progressing. Whenever you find that your mind is going into this kind of stillness, ask yourself, 'Whose mind is feeling this stillness?' Keep asking yourself that, till you reach the source of your enquiry. The question and answer both lie there.

V: But you often enter some type of samadhi.

M: I do not 'enter' any type of samadhi. The state I am in, is a constant state of samadhi, in which the mind has been completely killed.

V: Are there stages in which a seeker reaches such a samadhi?

M: Yes, I myself experienced the three stages of samadhi on this path. In the first stage, I found that with constant effort I could keep my mind in the absolute. However, with the least bit of disturbance, the mind would jump out into the world, and its habits or *vasanas* would exercise control. Then, as I progressed on the path a bit, I found that the mind would remain submerged for long periods without effort. I could view the world with equanimity and with a feeling of unity. However, even here, the mind was always present in the background. The memory of pleasure and pain had not lost their grip on me. This state, too, was not a permanent state.

V: And then ... ?

M: Finally, the mind just dissolved. When there was no mind, there were no habits to pull me into the conventional world. This was an irreversible change that came with realization.

V: What is this type of samadhi called?

M: It is called *Sahaja Nirvikalpa Samadhi*, the samadhi without effort. It is the natural state of the enlightened person, the Gyani. Once a person enters this, it is like a rebirth. He does not revert to his previous stage. As Nisargadutta Maharaj said, the fruit ripens slowly and, one day, just falls.

# A Happy God

My god is a happy god. He laughs with amusement at our deeds and with indulgence at our conceits. Sometimes, perhaps, he is mildly surprised at what we can do both above and below his expectation. But he is never angry. He has no call to be. By our misdeeds we do not threaten him, we threaten ourselves and probably make him chuckle at our self- importance and pomposity, as we may chuckle if a toy created by us acted peculiarly.

My god is perhaps amused that we mistake our state of mind for his, transfer our emotions to him and even assign 'Him' a gender and, often, a form. We give him myriad names and treat these names, thought up by us, special. He is amused that we act scared when we risk his anger in our imagination. He is perhaps also amused when we jump to 'defend' him, when nothing any of us can do can harm him even a little bit.

There are those amongst us who think that they speak for my god. Many of them are lying, either for gain for themselves in this world or hope of gain in the other one. Or, they are sincerely deluded into thinking that they are god's chosen ones, authorized to speak on his behalf to their fellow-men and women. These last are no less harmful or pointless than those who are knowingly hypocritical. Being saved from god's so-called anger is less urgent than being saved from their self-righteous wrath, which, usually, has more to do with their chosen path than with their averred destination.

My god has no reason to be angry, sarcastic or jealous. We are like infants for Him and no one except the impatient or immature would inflict these sentiments on infants; and god is certainly neither.

My god expects me to view his creation with an open and questing mind and live in it with lightness of spirit and vibrancy of feeling. Goodwill and tolerance are a part of his expectation. He views my progress towards him with the measure of how 'one' I feel with all that sprang from him. This oneness eventually leads to its source, himself, and is beyond any of our puny concepts of 'divinity' or 'holiness' or even 'bliss'. Those who touch even the edge of this oneness, realize that mankind has no word in any language that can do it justice. All our expectations of heaven fall severely short in its unending fulfilment.

There are only a very few women and men who have a right to speak of god, as he would want us to speak of him. These rare ones have tasted this 'oneness' in full measure. They shine like stars in our constellation and are marked by the unity of their thought and the benignity of their deeds. Though religions and rituals may have formed around them, these masters are beyond religion and rituals. The 'smile of god' shines through their own smile. When we are in tune with them, we can feel some of their great joy inside ourselves. And, if this happens to us when we get only a second-hand glimpse of god, imagine how happy he himself must be.

Yes, my god is a happy god. With the power to do whatever he wants, how can he be otherwise? Thus, I do not fear the wrath of god. I fear only the wrath of my own conscience which god put there. For, ultimately it is not god who will critically judge my actions. It is my own self.

## On Giving

Dharm prospers when we give back to society more than we receive. There is a shloka in Vivekananda Kendra's prayer:

जीवने यावदादानं स्यात् प्रदानं ततोऽधिकम् ।
इत्येषा प्रार्थनास्माकं भगवन् परिपूर्यताम् ॥

O Lord, please fulfil this wish of mine
That I can give back more than what I have received in my life

There are many who need our help through material things or other kinds of support. Let us, who have received so much in life, consider their plight compassionately. But, while doing so, we must remember one very important thing – we must remember to offer our gift with our palm upwards, literally and metaphorically, so that the other person does not feel like a beggar with his palm face up, asking for alms.

As I resolve to help others, at times I also feel the need to receive some gifts from you. What I need, my friend, in moments of sorrow and joy, is a smile from you that says you know how I feel. A dance for the song playing in my mind, a heartbeat full of understanding and the realization that you are wholeheartedly there for me, as I am there for you, both in moments that need uplifting and in times when we can laugh and enjoy life together.

Let us both add value to each other's lives, so that we have more to give to others, too.

# I Have Been a Tree and Some Other Things as Well

In my human-ness lie the memories of many other forms. I have been a cloud, floating in the sky, sometimes rubbing against other clouds creating lightning and thunder, at other times, wafting gently down verdant valleys.

I have been a tree, with my roots firmly in the ground of my land, nurtured by centuries of culture and history. My stem was the genes that I inherited from my parents, and my leaves were my arms, raised to the sunlight, seeking nurture.

I have been a bee, buzzing from master to master, from book to book, from video to video, imbibing knowledge and sometimes, sharing this honey with others in my hive. Now and then, I have helped hone the wisdom of some of my betters through my naïve interventions. If nothing, I have taught them patience.

I was a monkey once, jumping from branch to branch, tree to tree, in the hope of a better tomorrow. Then I acquired some wisdom. I learnt to try and make a better today and I found that I was a monkey no more.

I have been a turtle, hiding in my shell from unwelcome people and unworthy thoughts. I have been a fish swimming in the river of my own emotions, trying to avoid alluring hooks dangling in front of me. I have experienced hot water and cold, and in more felicitous times, calm water, at the perfect temperature. I would have loved to dwell there forever but, at that time in my life, this was but wishful thinking.

I have been an otter building dams so that my tribe could get sustenance, and find a home and a place to dance. I have been a tiger, showing my claws when my family was threatened.

I have been a hawk, soaring in the sky on wings of ambition, looking down for opportunities to grab in my talons. In my earlier years I have been tamed by a trainer, and I used to return to my perch on his hand at a fixed time every morning, but now I have freed myself from daily drudgery and am no one's slave.

Strangely, I have been a wolf, too, howling at the moon, urging it to give me some of its light so that I, too, could shine as gloriously as it did. But that did not last many moons, for I learnt that its light was borrowed, and it was merely a poseur. I did not howl during the day, because some silly things are easier done when the sun does not shine.

I have also been so many other things. However, I am thankful for some of the things I have never been. I was never a hyena, feeding on the carcass of someone's abnegation. I have never been a snake, speaking with a forked tongue, hoarding poison to use on whoever I thought were unworthy. I have not been its prey, a rat, nibbling greedily at everything I saw and spreading disease wherever I went.

I am thankful, too, for never having been a bean counter, who revels in counting someone else's treasure and keeps lauding them for their achievement, instead of focusing on his own.

Yes, indeed, I am thankful for never being any one of these. I am also thankful for what I see who I am now.

Years later, I have become a swan, floating on the still waters of life with my mate, serenely going to the other shore, in companionable silence, watching others become what they will, sometimes helping them with their own becoming. There are no time-tables in our lives now, no pressures from others, just togetherness.

In this calm, the imagination lives. I see incipient forms in me, yet to be born. These are gentler in nature but are waiting their turn, some of them with mild impatience. In the years to come, I am sure I will see some interesting ones emerge, as me, yet.

My final wish is to become a giver, a pair of open palms, turned upwards, offering components of my body when I have no use for them, as an organ donor. Let the warmth and vitality of these keep some others alive and well, so that they, too, can get a chance to be some of what I have revelled in becoming from time to time.

The components of my mind are already available through my prose and poetry for those who care to experience these. Perhaps, someone else will find his or her own other forms here.

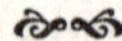

# The Asha Road

We have two paths ahead of us and one behind. The one behind us is the road we have travelled on, till the present. The left fork ahead of us is, for want of a better word, the Road of Reason, though one often comes across the unreasonable on it. The right fork is the one Zarathustra called Asha. These forks are there at any point of time, regardless of which road we are on.

Kwang Dze tells the following story which highlights the difference between the two paths.

"In what way does your Majesty, by the grace of heaven, exercise your mind?" Shun asked.

The reply was, "I simply show no arrogance towards the helpless; I do not neglect the poor people; I grieve for those who die; I love their infant children; and I am compassionate towards their widows."

Shun rejoined, "Admirable, as far as it goes; but it is not what is great."

"How then," asked Yao, "do you think I should do?"

Shun replied, "When a sovereign possesses the virtue of heaven, then when he shows himself in action, it is in stillness. The sun and moon simply shine, and the four seasons pursue their courses. So it is with the regular phenomena of day and night, and with the movement of the clouds by which rain is distributed."

Yao said, "Then I have only been persistently troubling myself! What you wish is to be in harmony with heaven, while I wish to be in harmony with men."

Those who wish to be in harmony with men are the ones travelling the road of reason in a compassionate and wise way. There are others on this road, too, who are not so wise. Those who want to be in harmony with heaven choose the road called Asha.

Asha means righteousness in Avestan. It means truth, too, and other things which cannot be translated. It also means 'hope' in Sanskrit, the ancient tongue of my people that is very similar to Avestan. Others have called this way Thien Tao, the path to heaven.

There is no real translation in English which can convey the full scope of these all-encompassing ancient words. We have to experience them to know. Then we do not need inadequate words to explain it.

On the road of reason, we find much scholarly debate and many other mundane things. There is a lot of noise on this road, both pleasing and jarring. Life is lived here in all its colours. Most of us choose to keep travelling on this road.

On the road called Asha, we find the five divine sparks of creation – Good Purpose (*Manah*, in Sanksrit, which can be translated as Will), Dominion or courage (*Vairya*), Devotion (*Spenta Armaiti*), Wholeness (*Haurvatat*) and Immortality (*Ameretat*). The last stage has been called *Baqa* by the Sufis and *Turiya* in the Upanishads. This does not refer to physical immortality and is another concept that can be better experienced than explained.

Kwang Dze says that vacancy, stillness, placidity, taste-lessness, silence and non-action are the qualities of those travelling the right road, and they would go on to perfection. The Upanishads also endorse this. The essence of this road is calm and balance. This road of righteousness leads to the creative principle itself.

The Upanishads have explained the divine's qualities in negatives – not (only) this, not (only) that, etc. since to define it in positive terms is to limit its scope. The traveller's state at the end of Asha can also be only so defined.

At the end of the Asha road, if I am to believe the Upanishads, the Hevajra Tantra and the Tibetan Book of the Dead, *Bardo Thodol*, I can say:

*Complete in myself, fully free*
*I am all that I can be*
*I am that all the time*
*I am its prose, I am its rhyme*
*Not for me pilgrimages galore*
*Or visits to seers door to door*
*Wherever I look, there I am*
*My holy land is where I am*

Let us introspect and decide which road we wish to be on. If we want to remain on the road of reason, we should try to be like Yao and strive to travel in harmony with men. If we wish to be on the Asha road, we should heed Shun's advice and strive to travel in harmony with creation, seeking our way in the calmness of inner and outer silence.

# The Caverns of the Religious

Imagine a huge cavern. Diverse creatures live in that cavern. There are bats, wrens, peacocks, sharks, whales, starfish, monkeys, lions, tigers, cats, hyenas, wolves, elephants, scorpions, snakes – think of any creature, and it is found in this cavern. All these creatures derive their sustenance from the cavern itself and are loyal to it.

Some of these creatures are peace-loving. Others are violent in nature. Some are talkative, others are quiet. Some cite the light, the glens and peaceful pools in the cavern, and consider it a heavenly place. Others let the thorny bushes, jagged rocks and poisonous plants shape their mindset.

There are many such caverns in Cavern-Land and the attitude of the denizens of each of these depends upon what is found inside the cavern. In caverns where the environment is, by and large, peace-loving, the creatures are more easy-going, fun-loving and tolerant of others. Those who live in caverns where there are many areas with arid deserts, jagged rocks and thorny bushes tend to be more intolerant. Those entering uninvited here are often resented.

When someone intrudes into these caverns, each resident responds according to its own cavern-view. The peaceful ones take it easy. The violent ones are inhospitable and try to eliminate the 'offender'.

The inhabitants of different caverns each swear that their cavern is the best. In some caverns there is a firm belief among the creatures that theirs is the ONLY cavern and all those who are outside it may as well be dead. Various pejorative names have been invented for these 'others'.

Sometimes, those living in the caverns fight among themselves. Some insist that their view from the place they live in is the correct one. Others say that we can see different things from where we are. Each is unwilling to see the other's point of view. Frequently, the result is violence. This happens in almost all caverns but more in those which have a large diversity of often contradictory geographic features such as green leas, deserts, violent oceans, peaceful lakes, mysterious grottos, and dark niches. Based on their conditioning, each selects what they wish to see. What they see, in turn, reinforces their conditioning. Usually, the meek suffer.

Is any particular cavern evil? Are all caverns inherently good, but misunderstood by some creatures living in them?

Neither of these questions has a simple 'yes' or 'no' answer. Instead, the appropriate answer is 'yes and no'. Yes, these caverns have both good and bad places where various residents find emotional succour. And no, no one is 'misguided'. It is just that some get their guidance from the ethos of their dark abodes within their cavern, and their behaviour is mediated by the nature of the specific place they chose to call their own.

Given this nature of the caverns and their residents, whenever some violence is perpetrated by those who live in the not-so-good places, there is pressure on the other residents to either defend this violence, or offer the excuse that those responsible do not understand the true nature of the cavern and are 'misguided'. Unfortunately, this denial does not result in any long-term solution of the problem, because it tries to paper over the real nature of their cavern.

Until the peace-loving denizens of the caverns admit to themselves that dark places really exist in their cavern and evil acts have been born in these, they are in no position to do anything to remove these places, and clean up their cavern. And, unless this is done, the evil within the caverns will continue to flourish and play havoc in Cavern-Land.

What, then, should the peace-loving creatures in each cavern do? Firstly, they should visit all places in their cavern open-mindedly for themselves – as against taking the word of others about these. For those who are willing to sincerely try, this is not very difficult. Detailed maps are available to everyone in every cavern.

They have to be attentive while visiting the dark places in their cavern and should not let their mindset be guided by the evil they see there. They should be willing to see the evil as evil and not try to hide these behind masks of 'holiness'.

It would be great if they can just wall off those places and allow no one to enter there. They can also stop teaching their children about these places. Unfortunately, this is not possible in most caverns, as no one has the authority to cut off any place. On the contrary, often paths to these dark places have been strengthened by their denizens through the ages. Moreover, as mentioned, ancient maps are available to everyone and someone or the other will find their niche in these places again, anyway.

On the other hand, they can educate their residents regarding the history of the cavern and how and when it was constructed. They can then point out that, with the passage of time, the cavern needs to be modified to suit changed circumstances. What was true hundreds of years back, is not true today, and the geography of the cavern can be moderated in light of the present.

They will feel resistance against their attempts, especially from those who find their comfort in the dark nooks and crannies of the caverns. These are the ones who generally swear by the antiquity of the maps and insist that they cannot be changed by anyone. However, if enough creatures resolve to do so, they can put the dark places of the cavern in their historical perspective, and show that it is goodness that needs to grow rather than evil. The ghosts of the past need no longer control their present and future.

If the above does not work, there is, of course, a third alternative. No, I do not mean they should move to another cavern. Instead, they should make a new cavern based on their own ethos and move there, leaving those in the old cavern to be eliminated by those against whom they commit violence. This does not need new maps – the old ones are already there. It just needs new engineering, so that the evil aspects are eliminated in the final plans for the new cavern.

The question is – do those living in well-lit areas in their cavern have any intention of acknowledging that dark places exist in their cavern and the courage to really to do anything to eliminate these? As long as they keep denying that such places exist at all, the answer to this would be a sad 'no' despite all their pronouncements to the contrary. Recognition of the problem is the first step towards the solution.

## Doors of the Mind

Imagine a vast hall in our minds. We spend our lives in this hall. There are many doors here and one corridor leading off, with a door that is always open. In the final stages of our lives, we go into this open corridor and, at its end, fall off this plane of existence. This note is not about what happens when we fall off at the end. It is about what happens when we spend our time in this central hall.

The doors in the hall are of different colours. Behind these doors we can find creativity, laughter, adventure, love, serenity and fulfilment. There are some doors behind which we find negativity, too, in the form of addiction, disease, enmity, vileness and such things. When we open a door, we spend time behind it experiencing whatever that room contains. We then come out into the hall and have the choice to do nothing, open another door or go into the same one again. Inside these doors, there are other doors leading to different rooms, too.

All the doors are unlocked and open smoothly when we are born. Those we choose to ignore become harder to open, as their hinges rust. Those doors which we keep opening frequently remain smooth. In the nature of things, it is possible to be behind more than one door at the same time, but the time spent behind any additional door takes away the time from other doors.

As we age, we make our choices. We open certain doors and ignore others. We are guided in our choices by a variety of factors – our genes shape these to a certain extent. Our family and friends are another influence, for we usually prefer to open those doors behind which we are likely to find those we like or which are recommended by them. That is why the wise recommend good company, satsang.

When we spend too much time behind a particular door, the hinges start rusting and it becomes increasingly difficult to come out. Sometimes we spend too much time behind a door because we find happiness there – this may be a positive happiness or a negative one such as that caused by drugs. At other times, trauma keeps us there and we spend too much time behind a specific door because we feel helpless. This can happen because of things like prolonged illness, addiction, wrong company, or just because of prolonged social crises such as the recent Covid one. It can also happen because of laziness and lack of courage. Sometimes it happens because of our belief in our own importance. 'What will happen to all this if I leave?' is a question often asked and then replied in a way which enforces the sense of one's indispensability.

At all times, we must remember that in the final analysis, the choice is entirely ours. We are the openers of the doors. We can exercise our will and discretion. The hall belongs to us and it is not the other way around.

Whoever thinks that they belong to the hall are powerless to do anything worthwhile and prematurely await their end near the entrance of the open corridor. Ennui and a sense of worthlessness are the major experiences if one tarries at this point too long. Some people mistake this inaction for spiritual detachment but such people do not find the bliss they are looking for. They have refused to open the door which leads to bliss for whatever reason and mistake idle inaction for spirituality. They do not realize that true spirituality is behind a special door and it is full of inclusiveness, empathy and compassion. Usually this want of understanding is caused by the lack of inclination, lack of knowledge and sometimes even lack of proper guidance.

All of us need to introspect as to the doors we have opened, those we have shied away from, and those we would still like to open. We also need to think about whether we have become prisoners held in stasis by our own selves behind any particular door.

At the end of our lives, all the doors will open by themselves, but by then it would be too late. At that time the doors only allow us to go out into the hall, where the open corridor awaits.

There is one exception to this rule. This is the door marked spirituality. This room can sometimes be accessed through the room which is entered through the door marked religion. However, in most cases, people entering the door marked religion are unable to reach the spiritual, as they get engrossed in the many diversions offered by in the religion-room. In this room, religious leaders of different persuasions can be seen in every corner trying to beguile people by selling their particular charms and maps highlighting their own chosen ways. An impression has been conveyed by these religious leaders over the ages that we must enter the room of religion for the creator to listen to us because he does not do so in other places. This misunderstanding also tends to make the seeker unwilling to leave the varied attractions of this room by opening the door of spirituality, which can also be seen, clearly marked, in this room.

This door of spirituality leads to a wondrous corridor which, if travelled till the end, takes one outside this construct altogether, and permits the adept to view it from the perspective of the one who created it all. The adept realizes what has been called moksha, satori, enlightenment and baqa. At the end of her life, the realized one might experience a change of form but not a change of focus. She finds herself at the place she already was. This state has to be experienced and cannot be learned through words. As one must see for oneself what colour is, and it is not possible to describe it in words to a blind person, so it is with this state.

We should review the choices we have made till now. We should also evaluate if we have been behind a particular door for too long. If need be, we should make fresh choices before the door hinges on the unopened doors get too rusted to open. Remember, till we have the power to choose, it is not too late to open any new door. It may be increasingly difficult to do so, but, with a strong will, it is still possible. We only have to exercise our will in channels which it has not travelled to before. The alternative is travelling through the door-less corridor to our end, carrying with us the regret of what could have been.

Happy journey.

# A Wondrous Journey

A grape, fresh off the vine, its white powdery bloom, a badge of freshness, partly hiding its smiling surface. So many possible futures hiding in its smooth skin bursting with juice, its sensual roundness a treat for the eyes and the touch. The delicious taste of nature at its best.

A grape, carefully nurtured over the years, liquid manna, adding cheer to my life. Its acidity tempered, as if by inner wisdom, its full body alluring to the tongue. I look at its vibrant colour, refracting the light, much lovelier than before, I smell the beautiful bouquet that its journey has endowed and wonder, humbled.

A grape, transformed into a sparkling elixir, tickling the nose, synonymous with celebrations, a smile in a glass. Its components in perfect balance, the colour of purity.

A grape, fermented and double distilled in well-designed copper alembic stills, and aged in oak casks, a treat for the eyes and the palate, warming the insides on cold nights.

And, in a few years, a grape, well-preserved, sweeter than ever, a beautiful raisin. Each small wrinkle a testament to its becoming. As I hold it in my hand, I revel in its softness and smile in anticipation. In little bites, I savour the lovely flavour of the deliciousness that the grape has evolved into.

I close my eyes and fondly contemplate all these that I have come across during the last five decades. I find a figure slowly forming in my mind, embodying all these qualities. I see in it the freshness of a new grape, the colour, aroma and complexity of a rare wine, the laughter and good cheer of a champagne, the warmth and depth of a cognac and the wonderful sweetness of a raisin.

I wonder how it can be possible for such beautiful diversity to exist all at once. I look closely and find that the figure is that of my best friend and companion, in all her sweetness, depth and wisdom. I know, then, that this miracle can indeed happen.

A wondrous journey indeed.

# I Visited Kahlil Gibran Today

I visit old friends now and then. Sometimes it is Yajnavalkya, sometimes Rumi, sometimes Rabiya al Adawiyya, sometimes Angelus Silesius, sometimes Lao Tzu. I call them old friends because in their presence, I do not feel like the 'other'.

Today, I met Kahlil Gibran, whose words are like flower petals floating gently on the Ganges of my mind.

There was much that he had to say. I also understood him in the gaps between the words, when nothing was said. I give below just a very small part of what he told me in the *Garden of the Prophet*, in the hope that you, too, will find it of relevance.

He said,

'It is only when you are lost in your smaller selves that you seek the sky which you call God. Would that you might find paths into your vast selves; would that you might be less idle and pave the roads!'

'My mariners and my friends, it were wiser to speak less of God, whom we cannot understand, and more of each other, whom we may understand. Yet I would have you know that we are the breath and the fragrance of God. We are God, in leaf, in flower, and oftentimes in fruit.'

and,

'The angels are tired of the clever. And it was but yesterday that an angel said to me: "We created hell for those who glitter. What else but fire can erase a shining surface and melt a thing to its core?"

And I said: "But in creating hell you created devils to govern hell." But the angel answered: Nay, hell is governed by those who do not yield to fire.'

Then Al Mustafa said: 'My friends and my road-fellows, pity the nation that is full of beliefs and empty of religion.'

This reminded me of so many nations and of ours, too. Then he said something else that also reminded me of my own Bharat. He added, 'Pity the nation that acclaims the bully as a hero, and that deems the glittering conqueror bountiful.' And I heard, 'Pity the nation that acclaims a media celebrity as a hero and the corrupt leader bountiful.'

He then told me, 'Pity the nation divided into fragments, each fragment deeming itself a nation.' And I heard, 'Pity the nation divided into states, each state deeming itself a nation.'

At one point I heard him say, 'My soul is running over with the wine of the ages. Is there no thirsty one to come and drink?'

Hearing this, I exclaimed, "*Ana huna, ya Mustafa*!" He looked at me and I looked at him and we burst out laughing; a bubbling laughter that welled unbidden from inside. "Yes, you are here, friend. I know you feel the thirst but you know as well as I, that my wine needs a thirst deeper than what you have at this time."

"I know, that, Mustafa," replied I, "but as my thirst is now, it is fulfilled by just being in your presence. When that time comes when my thirst is deep enough to partake of all your wine, you and I will be mist together and your wine will also be mine."

Al Mustafa just smiled. And so it went. The hour I spent with Al Mustafa flew past magically, with ideas singing in my mind and feelings dancing in my heart.

No cameras are allowed in the continuum where I meet these friends, else I would have posted a selfie with him. For now, let his words suffice.

# An Ancient Peepal Tree Told Me This about My 'Tree Rings'

It was a very large and ancient tree. Its trunk would need at least six people holding hands to encircle. As I sat under it, resting my head against the ecru bark, I looked up at the magnificent canopy above me, in many shades of green. The atmosphere was mystical under it. It is no wonder that this tree is called Ficus Religiosa, the sacred ficus, I idly thought, as my consciousness drifted away into serenity.

Suddenly I heard a soft chuckle. I looked around but there was no one there.

"Don't worry, it is only me, the Peepal you are sitting under," the voice appeared to come from somewhere in my mind.

"You can talk?" I said, surprised.

The Peepal chuckled again, "What do you think?" it asked.

I mulled over this and then said, "That's wonderful. I was just thinking about your name."

"Aah," said the voice, "Ficus Religiosa! Yes, I am also called Peepal, Pippal, Bodhi Tree and Ashwattha. The Kannadas call me Arali and the Japanese call me Indo bodaiju. So many other names, too. None of these names make any difference to me. You humans have a way of labelling everything and then confining its existence within the limitations of your own label."

"What do you mean?" I asked confused.

"You think I am especially auspicious. Know that every tree is sacred, every leaf an homage to the divine. There is nothing special about me, despite what you have attributed to me. None of you would be alive if there were no plants and trees. We make it possible for you to get rain water, your food and the very air that enables you to live."

"But Gautam Buddha achieved his enlightenment under a tree like you," I said.

"You think the tree you call Bodhi had something to do with it?" the Peepal said, laughing. "It was Gautam's achievement, not ours. My fellow tree just happened to be there when Gautam needed a place to sit. His time had come. He could have sat anywhere—in a cave, for example, as others have done—and become the Buddha. He is the one who is sacred."

"And, one more thought for you. You know that a branch from the original Peepal under which Gautam sat was planted in Anuradhapura in Sri Lanka centuries back – the one you call Jaya Sri Maha Bodhi. Ask yourself how many others have gained enlightenment under that tree? Ask yourself how many have got enlightened at Bodhgaya itself? If your answer is 'none' then you will know who was responsible for Buddha's enlightenment."

"But Krishna also said in the Gita," I didn't want to give up, "I am the Peepal tree among the trees, Narada among the sages, Chitraratha among the Gandharvas and sage Kapila among the Siddhas." I paused and added, "Your seeds are used for prayer beads, you are also helpful in so many diseases. You are indeed special."

I sensed a smile. "If you say so, but I do not wish to argue this with you. We trees do not argue. We just are!"

"So you are not sacred?" I asked.

The tree laughed; a deep laugh that seemed to echo from another world. "As I said, every tree is sacred. I am the same, no more, no less."

While I was mulling over this, a thought occurred to me and I asked, "Don't you get bored standing in one place for your entire life?"

"I have seen the earth circle the sun eighteen hundred times." There was amusement in Peepal's voice, "I have not been bored for even one leaf-flutter during this period."

The tree paused and then resumed, "You move here and there for your survival and for giving meaning to your life. I stay in one place and watch the world move. The very air I breathe is full of stories – from your outbreath I can make out what your mood is, even what you ate. Birds, bees and animals who pass by or live near me, gossip all the time about their interesting lives. Fireflies come at night and show me their beauty. The night owl talks of its exploits, monkeys of theirs. My roots have fungi and bacteria that interact with other trees and help me exchange messages with other trees. I lead a rich life. How can I get bored?"

"I see," I said, "I had not thought of you like this."

"I even keep a diary," the tree said, amused, "and it is perhaps more comprehensive than your diary."

"A diary?" I asked, "and where do you write?"

"In my tree rings. I have a record of every year for the last eighteen hundred years. It shows how the weather was, how the air was and how the water was. If there were storms or a volcano erupted, you can find a record here."

As I was thinking about this, the voice said, "All of us have these rings, you know. Even you."

"My memories, you mean?" I asked.

"Indeed," it said, "but more than that, every part of your body is a record of your life, the liver you misused, the calcium deposit in your arteries, the dead hair follicles, the condition of your lungs that breathe polluted air, your heart that you stress unwisely, your gut bacteria—everything is akin to my rings. You should visit them some time."

As I was thinking about this, the tree said, "Yes, and the good things too—the remembered laughter, the feeling of mystical joy, the energy in your muscles, the happiness at seeing your children and grandchildren smile, the creativity, the anticipation of meeting loved ones—there are so many wonderful rings in your life, too."

"I have spoken more than I usually do," it added, "I will speak no more. You think about your own sacredness, not mine. I wish you well. Goodbye."

The presence vanished from my mind. In the sudden silence, I was acutely conscious of the fluttering of some leaves above me as a bird with shiny green feathers landed on its nest. I could hear the skittering sound of bugs near the tree roots. A bee buzzed looking for nectar. Two squirrels climbed down the tree trunk chirping companionably and headed for some fallen seeds. A fly with iridescent wings came and sat on my arm and then flitted away. Some ants marched busily near me, seeking their sustenance. A leaf gently floated down and landed on my head – a blessing from 'my' Peepal. I smiled.

A cool breeze made the canopy ripple and brought me back into this world from the Peepal's world. I felt that the tree had such a rich life and, in its mirror, I could see that I, too, had a similar one, with my own nestlings, my own bees, my own bugs and my own squirrels. And indeed, my own fireflies. Yes, I must visit my own rings more often and see how the new ones that I make are more radiant.

And respect all trees as sacredly vibrant.

# Beyond the Walls of Memories & Concepts

We are familiar with the saying that a frog in the well thinks that the entire world exists within that well. Many of us will be surprised to learn that we, too, spend our whole lives living in wells of our own.

Our wells have two walls. The inner wall of our 'world-well' is built of memories. The mortar used in this wall is created by our habits, and this wall is painted with our emotions.

The wall of memories is reinforced by the wall of concepts that encircles it.

Our subjective reality is inside these walls. Beyond these lies objective reality. Since the mind creates these walls and jealously guards them, it is not possible to go past them till the mind is active.

A still mind enables us to go beyond the wall of memories, and we see the world in a new light. However, a still mind is necessary but not sufficient to go past the wall of concepts.

The still mind understands others much better than it does when it is burdened by memories. However, they are still 'others'. This 'me' and 'you', 'I', 'he' and 'she' are primary concepts that remain alive in the still mind.

A root concept is at the foundation of the wall of concepts – "I am this mind and this body is mine." Concepts that condition our mind are built on this foundation. Religious conditioning, which uses equal measures of greed and fear, is part of the brick and mortar of this second wall. So is social conditioning.

The wall of concepts is not easy to breach. Our very existence appears to hinge on its foundations remaining intact. If I am not this mind, then who am I? The mind cannot answer this question, for, when it is still, it is inactive, and if it starts to answer this, it is no longer still. The eyes cannot see themselves.

All is not lost, however. There is a portal to take us beyond the wall of concepts. Its door is through the spiritual heart, slightly to the right of the breast-bone.

I can see some who have indulged me this far sigh and leave at this stage. They are the rationalists who are wary of anything that their instruments cannot quantify. They are firmly committed to living within their well. Let me address myself to those who are more open-minded.

Yes, the portal is through the spiritual heart, also called the Anahat Chakra. When someone with a still mind is able to drain all their concepts into the spiritual heart, symbolized by the chakra of the unstruck sound, they succeed in going beyond the wall of concepts. It is not easy, but, with faith and patience, it is possible. In the case of many seers, the power of the primal life force—the Kundalini—rises from the Muladhar Chakra to the Sahasrara Chakra and is then drained here in the Anahat Chakra, sweeping all concepts ahead of it.

When we are out of the wall of concepts and memories, we exist in the 'real' world. The concepts are still there and the memories, too. The realized seer is not comatose. But these are seen from the outside for what they are – artificial constructs created by the mind for survival. The foundation built to resist assault from the inside can do nothing if it is assaulted from the outside.

Beyond the wall of concepts, the possessive 'I' of the body-mind is no more, and its perspective of 'he' and 'she' and 'me', 'mine' and 'hers' are gone. The concept of time, so beloved of rationalists, is also not present here, nor is God, adored by the conventionally religious.

In this bold, timeless, objective world anything is possible.

I am aware of all this and I still keep living within my walls of memories and concepts. Such is the power of the mind and its fear of dissolution. This can only be overcome, either when one is impelled by one's accumulated karma or *prarabdha,* or through the guidance of an enlightened seer.

# Who are the Tenants Living in Your Mind?

Imagine that you are the owner of a multi-storey building with many apartments. You live on the ground floor and have tenants living in the other apartments. Some of them have been living there since you were an infant. Others have been invited by you to live there. You are familiar with a number of these tenants but there are some even you do not know about. They have sneaked in under your subconscious and are now occupying one or more apartments.

Some of these tenants are angelic and some are devilish. Some are inherently so while others are one or the other depending upon the circumstances. All of them produce drugs in their apartments and put these drugs in your overhead water tank which supplies your water. The devilish ones also invite their friends and sympathizers to come and live with them and help them in their mischief.

One example of a tenant who has started living in your apartment building when you were very small is this. At the age of three, you had bent down to pet a dog and it bit you. That experience settled this particular tenant in one of your apartments. Every time you come close to a dog, this tenant blows his trumpet, disturbing your peace.

There are so many such tenants living there.

Then there are others who you have actively invited to live in your building. You went on social media and started following their posts. Or, you met someone and became close friends. When you do this, you lay out a welcome mat for them and they come and settle in one of your apartments.

When these tenants mix their drugs in your water supply, you feel different emotions. These range from affection, elation, anger, angst, anguish, annoyance, anxiety, apathy, arousal, awe all the way down to terror, trust, wonder, worry etc. via euphoria, grief, hysteria, etc.

Yes, your moods are shaped by what is mixed in your water, coming down from the overhead tank of your cognitive apartment. The quality of this water depends entirely on the tenants you have, since they have free access to your water supply and they use it at will.

What are the drugs that these tenants mix in your water? They are the hormones that your body's endocrine glands produce, and send to other parts of the body through your bloodstream – your water pipeline. These hormones are essential for your survival and are finely regulated by the body's natural mechanism. However, when these tenants visit the endocrine glands, they over-produce whatever hormone they are addicted to, and the effects can be disastrous.

Let us take one example. Suppose one of your tenants is someone you follow on social media who is always fulminating against something or the other. He visits your adrenal gland, and hacks it to produce excess cortisol, adrenaline and other hormones.

Similar in nature to the above tenant, there could be another one who is always busy with conspiracy theories, which make you fearful. This tenant also mixes more cortisol and adrenaline in your pipeline than your system needs.

When excessive quantities of these 'drugs' enter your pipeline and reach the ground floor—your brain—you feel anger, fear, stress and other similar symptoms. Your heart rate goes up, you may even start sweating. You may live in a constant state of apprehension. The government is out to get you, there are groups that will destroy the world, there are kidnappers everywhere, you are not good enough, and so on. This also reduces the blood flow to the prefrontal cortex, and this makes your thinking foggy. The excess adrenaline makes you live in a state of fight or flight. And these are just two of the many hormones that you have which can be hijacked by these tenants. Not something to wish for.

If you owned an actual physical apartment building and had such tenants, wouldn't you like to pay them a visit? I recommend that you visit your cognitive tenants, too, now and then. Make a list of those you can recognize, and write down the emotion that they are promoting in you. If you find 'anger', 'rage', 'fear', 'depression', and other similar negative emotions arising because of any of them, highlight their names and give them an eviction notice.

In practical terms, take the case of someone on your social media timeline. You never feel joy on reading their posts. Why have them on your timeline? Why follow such a person?

You may have a friend who is always negative, casting a shadow on your life whenever you interact. Why keep them as a tenant?

While the recent tenants can be recognized and dealt with, there are other older ones—those you acquired during your infancy and childhood—who are not so easily evicted. They are so well entrenched that you take them for granted. Often it needs a trained psychologist even to point out that they are alive and well, and creating mischief inside you.

Having said that, it is possible to identify at least some of them by noticing and analysing your reactions to some stimuli, that are uncharacteristic for you. When you look deeper, you may find at least some of these ghostly tenants lurking behind these reactions.

Being aware of such tenants is half the battle won. The second half, evicting them from your building, can sometimes be ensured by you without professional help if you are determined, and if you have someone to talk to. It so happens that such ghosts do not like open air – talking about them with someone wise who you implicitly trust, often evicts them from your apartment. However, there will be some die-hard ones and evicting them may need the expertise of trained therapists. Professional help should be sought if the nastiness of the tenants is dire enough to endanger your health or life.

Apart from the above, there is another reason why it is important to evict undesirable tenants. *They often pose as the landlord when you are overwhelmed by their hormone overload.* This makes you appear as someone who you really are not.

Spiritual Gurus say that to achieve enlightenment, you need to evict all the tenants residing in your apartment. That is not an easy quest. However, all of us can make a start by recognizing and evicting the undesirable ones to start with.

# What Will the Stories of Your Life Be?

Your life talks to the world around you every moment of your existence. Just pause and consider – what is your life saying? What stories is it telling others? What impression is it conveying to the world about you, the author, the lead actor and the hero of your epic?

Hearing what your life has to say, will those listening yawn? Will they sneer? Will they laugh with amusement? Will they laugh with derision? Will they be full of wonder? Will they be inspired? Will they learn about things to do and things to avoid? Will they remember? And, if they do, will the memory make them happy or leave them unhappy?

Every life story is unique, and yours is, too. What will it be? It is up to you to decide that.

Just remember a few of things about these stories.

Unlike when you tell stories, the stories told by your life cannot be manipulated. Oh yes, you can fool a few people for a while but, eventually, when your epilogue is written, the fake CV you presented to the world is of no value. It is how you actually lived, and what you actually did, that counts.

Secondly, your life tells a different story to every listener. The story your son is hearing from your life is different from the story your husband or wife or father or mother is hearing. Similarly, every friend—no, every person—you meet, hears a different story.

In these stories you may sometimes feature as kind, at other times for the same person or for someone else, as unkind. Often you play the part of a hero but sometimes you are a villain for someone. You can come across as loving or as cold, a happy presence lighting up someone's life or a depressing one conveying doom and gloom. Even, perhaps a fearsome one, making someone cringe.

As I mentioned earlier, it is up to you to choose your role in the story that your life tells.

Some traits such as wisdom, integrity, compassion, dependability, a sense of fun, talent, creativity etc. help project you more as a hero than a villain. If your life story does not include these traits, remember that they are worth cultivating.

One more thing. The story that your life tells others may often be perceived differently by different people, even if it is the same story. This is because their perception will depend upon their own emotional filters. How they perceive your stories will be coloured by what the story their life tells.

At this stage some may ask, "Why should I bother what stories my life is telling others? How does it matter to me? I am ME – an independent, free-thinking individual and I will make my own life as it suits me." A common thought but not a worthy one.

You are not the only member of your species on this planet. You depend upon others for keeping you alive and functioning. Think of the electricity you use, the water you drink, the clothes you wear, the food you eat, the interaction you have with your family, your friends, your foes, and with countless people you pass by in your life-journey. Unless you are a hermit, all these things and so many more involve other humans. You are not independent, except in the eyes of your ego. Whether you like it or not, you are connected to thousands of others by threads often not of your making.

Among these are the people paying attention to the stories your life is telling them. Even if you are a hermit, living alone in a cave, your life is not silent. It is conveying something about you to others.

So, when you say that you do not care about what others think about you, your life tells the audience, "Look at me! I am an egoistic jerk, only concerned about my own well-being. To hell with all of you!"

On the contrary, when you extend your hand and your heart to someone, your life tells that person, "I am here for you. You can depend on me if you need me."

You have to decide which of these stories you want your life to tell.

This is an example of the choice between black and white alternatives but you have countless other hues on your palette. I hope you will select with care.

May the stories others hear from your life be uplifting ones, full of joy that make them smile every time they think of you and warm them when they are feeling cold.

## The Messages We Are

We are born as blank sheets of papers, you and I, with envelopes addressed to no one. Over time, we become messages, of love for some, and of hate for others, of boredom and excitement, of joy and woe. Some of us, needing envelopes no more, become origami-like, that everyone can see and applaud.

Some messages have reached the names on the envelopes and caused happiness, sorrow, anger, surprise, even amazement and admiration. Others, like unrequited love, still lie undelivered, their stories unread.

When we have the time to look back, let us read the messages we have written on the papers that we are, and the names on the envelopes we meant these for. Perhaps there is still time to edit some of the messages to make them more joyful, or maybe erase the names on some envelopes.

This is important for these are magical messages that will persist long after the paper is no more, and these are what we will be remembered by, in this world and that.

# 'My' Desires

I always say 'my desire'. Desire laughs at this presumption for it knows the truth. It is not 'my' desire. I belong to it and exist to serve its demands.

Yes, 'my' desire does not do my bidding; I do what it wants me to do. It doesn't suffer the consequences of my actions in doing as it wills. I do.

Desire is a capricious master. Once I fulfil its diktat, I expect it to fade away. But no. Sated, it grows bigger. And bigger again. And I, fool that I am, keep working to feed what I think is 'my' desire.

I know all this and yet keep faithfully role-playing in scripts written by my desires. Old ones remain and new ones keep getting born and I spend my life serving all of them like a bonded labourer.

Desires are clever. They do not try to master my logical self. Instead, they manipulate the part of me that is amenable to their manipulation – my ego. They convince it that its fulfilment lies in their fulfilment. What the ego doesn't realize is, that since the desires are never satisfied, the ego isn't, too. All it gets is crumbs, which leave it hungrier for more. It never learns.

It is not only 'ordinary folk' like me who do not know when enough is enough, and when they should stop being played by their puppet-masters. People far more eminent than me have spent their lives blindly working for their insatiable desires. Legendary people like Julius Caesar and Alexander the 'Great' are prime examples. "I won a great victory today, now to conquer the next country" drove them throughout their lives. Then there are the very rich, untiringly working to fulfil their desire's order to get richer still.

My logical mind knows this but the prime directive, so to say, of desires, is, *"Thou shalt ignore thy logical mind"*. However, therein lies redemption, too. I only have to disobey the prime directive.

This is easier said than done. Desires are experts at manipulating the ego. They convince it that if I do not get a car that is better than my neighbour's, I will be shamed. They make it believe that if I stop at ten million and my classmate has fifteen, I am a craven loser.

Most of us can never get out of these traps. Make the next million, buy the better car, conquer the next country...each of us has his or her indenture spelt out by desire, depending on personal predilections and circumstances. However, some fortunate ones are exceptions. They have realized the reality of this master-servant relationship and do not like it.

There are some who try to get out of this gradually. Okay, I'll start having one cigarette less, or I'll stop when I make the next million. They soon realize that desires are like seeds. If you try to merely bury them, they grow back with a vengeance. The only way to get rid of these master-monsters is to exterminate them, starting with their handmaiden, the ego.

The quickest way of doing this is through the counsel of an enlightened Master, a wise Guru, followed by meditation. The ego is strong and reluctant to let go, and the Master is needed to guide one onto a better path through his wisdom and grace.

Meditation is needed to walk further on this path. Properly and sincerely practiced, it puts the matter in perspective and gives primacy to the logical mind. It shows the ego its rightful place – that it needs to be only strong enough to ensure survival and not even a bit more to support any desire. Meditation makes one ready for fulfilment of the kind that is never possible through attempts to fulfil desires.

Some may say that seeking such spiritual fulfilment is also a desire. They would be wrong. While desires push towards their fulfilment, spiritual fulfilment pulls one into its fold. There is no desire associated with it because there is no ego associated with it. Spiritual fulfilment needs no seconds, so to speak. It stands alone.

Those who have felt this pull will realize of what I speak. Those who haven't may benefit from heeding the above and try to find a master who will help separate the grain from the chaff.

## Like Me, You Too Are a Wave

An epiphany...

Electrons, photons and others like them, when shot through a double slit, appear wavelike. However, if one observes which slit they pass through, they appear to be particles. The act of observation collapses the wave and 'changes' its state for the observer.

While this has been experimentally confirmed for fundamental particles, we also exhibit the same behaviour, even though we are on quite another scale of existence. In 'reality', we are like waves. When observed by others we are particle-like discrete objects.

The same holds true when we observe ourselves. Yes, when we keep evaluating ourselves, we become discrete objects, even for ourselves.

When we are devoid of judgmental observations, as in deep meditation, we become our wave-selves. Then we spread out to encompass all creation. When this happens, we find that the un-judged creation, too, is like a wave. Together, we reach a state of resonance and neither the world, nor us, remains what we were when being observed.

This state is called Turiya. Turiya, which means 'fourth' in Sanskrit, is pure consciousness. Turiya is what underlies our wave form. It is beyond the three states of waking, dreaming and dreamless deep sleep.

What does it mean in practice? Sitting in my garden, observing a tree, I find that it is separate from myself. I am aware of the duality of 'me' and the 'other'. Both the observer and the observed are in the particle state.

In our wave form, this duality dissolves and the tree and I become one. There are no leaves then, no stem, and no eyes seeing them. This feeling is entirely experiential and cannot be explained in words.

The objective of spiritual practice is to reach this state through stilling the judgmental mind that observes and evaluates everything around us, and by doing so, turns them into particulate objects in images of its own making.

Some may be confused by this because they have read in spiritual texts, 'Be a Witness' and taken it literally. If one is a 'witness' isn't one witnessing and will this not cause the wave function to collapse?

I would like to insert a smiley here. No, it will not cause the wave function to collapse because the term 'witness' is used in an entirely different context in this case.

'Witness' in this context does not mean the eyes that see, the ears that hear, the nose that smells, the tongue that tastes or the hand that touches. It does not even mean the mind that perceives or analyses. 'Witness' in this context is the real self, which is who we are. The 'vision' of this self is metaphorically spoken of as the 'witness' in the Upanishads. The Sanskrit word for 'witness' in this context is sakshi. This has been explained by Swami Sarvapriyananda, in this way: The awareness which experiences the mind from within; that awareness which cannot be objectified. Because it witnesses, shines upon, illumines every movement of the mind, every thought, every idea, every memory, every feeling, for want of a better term, it is called the witness.

Being a sakshi does not mean that we will actually see or feel something specific. Indeed, 'witnessing' is not seeing or feeling. It is Being.

In *Brihadaranyaka Upanishad,* (3.4.2), replying to Usasta's query on witnessing, Yajnavalkya says, "You cannot see that which is the witness of vision; you cannot hear that which is the hearer of hearing; you cannot think that which is the thinker of thought; you cannot know that which is the knower of knowledge. This is your Self that is within all; everything else but this is perishable."

Hearing this, Usasta, the son of Cakra, remains silent. Like him, let us remain silent, too, and meditate on the wave-form that we are.

## On Contentment

Spiritual contentment which comes with enlightenment is not complacence. Most people tend to confuse the two. Let me elaborate.

A complacent person is self-satisfied. He is too intellectually inactive and physically lazy to strive for anything. He convinces himself that he is satisfied with whatever he has and, thus, there is no need to really try for anything else. Alternately, he leaves everything to God, destiny or some other power which, he feels, governs his life.

Many people think that this is the epitome of spiritual attainment. It is primarily this misunderstanding that has been the undoing of India. However, spiritual enlightenment and such an attitude are diametrically opposed to each other. The complacent person keeps reality out by psyching himself into thinking that the world does not matter and that he has moved beyond worldly desires. In a sense, a complacent person builds walls around himself. The truly spiritually awakened person, on the other hand, breaks all walls between himself and the world. For such a person, worldly desires remain no more, not because they are beneath him, or because he has suppressed them, but because having become one with the world, there is nothing left to desire.

There are as many kinds of people in the world. However, in terms of striving for results, we can broadly find people in three categories. Let me explain through an example.

Three people are fishing in a pond. The first has the normal ego-driven mentality. The second is the complacent type. The third is an enlightened seer.

The first raves and rants when he does not catch fish. He blames his equipment, his wife and his stars. He sits there with turmoil in his mind. He derives satisfaction from the fact that others haven't caught any, too. If he catches some fish, he compares these with what others have caught and is unhappy if his catch is less or if his fish are smaller. If his catch is more, he crows with satisfaction. In either case, he strives to get more the next time.

The 'complacent' fisherman who has not caught any fish, spends the day reading and drinking and, at the end of it, sighs, withdraws his line, collects his belongings and goes home, thinking that this is what his destiny is, and he cannot help it if he did not catch any fish. He will not try any better the next time, as he has convinced himself that his destiny is not in his own hands. He is not sure of what he wants and is too lazy to make the effort to find out and do something about it. He is fatalistic and will remain a loser, both in the spiritual and the materialistic sense.

The 'enlightened' fisherman lives every moment he is on the pond in a state of 'super-consciousness'. He feels the wind on his face, not only from the point of view of the fisherman but also of the wind. He sees himself as part of his boat, he finds himself revelling in every wave on the pond. He flies with every bird on the water. And what of the fish? He is there on the pond. Knowing this, the fish will come to him like iron to a magnet*, for they sense that he is a part of them. And, because of that, he will not have a hook or bait on his line. He does not need these. And his 'line', too will be just his conscious will, not coarse thread. Substitute 'money', 'followers', whatever else you wish, for 'fish' and you have the situation prevailing in our world today.

---

* This is literally true, also. It has been found that animals have an affinity with the enlightened people. For example, monkeys used to cluster around Ramana Mahrashi and keep still if he told them to. The same can be seen in the case of many other enlightened people, too.

All three fishermen will go home at the end of the day. The first, ego-driven fisherman, will be in a foul mood if he has not caught any fish, or if he has caught less than others, kicking his dog and making his and everyone else's life miserable. If he has caught more than others, he will boast about this to everyone he meets. The second will go home and sleep complacently. The third is at home wherever he is, and he will continue to enjoy the bliss of *being* equally intensely everywhere.

The 'awakened' one will not worry about how many fish the others have caught. He will remain steadfast as a rock in the solid realization that the fish which are there are also as much a part of him as the other fishermen, the pond, the boat and everything else in the world. This state is so different from the 'normal' that others might think of him as a madman or may confuse him with the complacent fisherman. They would be wrong to do so.

The successful spiritual seeker awakens to the world in a manner which cannot be described in words. He finds a fullness which is joyful, a bliss which is alive. He *becomes* the world. He and the world are in constant interaction at the primary level. The complacent person, on the other hand, skims over the world, ignoring it and thinking that he is pursuing a spiritual life. In fact, he and the world are charting a path indifferent to each other.

Regretfully, the spiritual quest has been misunderstood by most seekers on a number of fronts. One of these is their understanding of what is needed to 'kill' desire. Another is their understanding of what constitutes spiritual contentment.

On the first point, they tend to think that once they can avoid or 'overcome' temptation, they are well advanced on the spiritual path. Thus, they try to reduce temptation in their lives – by going into isolated retreats, by not seeing the faces of women, by not eating certain proscribed foods, by trying to censor things around them so that the 'evil' world does not make them waver from their path. Such people fool themselves into thinking that they can avoid temptation by not coming across it. However, this is not the way to go beyond temptation. There are no bypasses that allow one to avoid temptation on the road of life, if desires are present in the mind in a sleeping state. Such avoidance can, at best, keep desires asleep, but the moment temptation comes in view, desires will definitely awaken.

On the matter of contentment, many seekers think that once they can feel complacent about their lives, they are content. True spiritual contentment is not dead complacence. It is alive and creative. This is the difference between repeating 'Aham Brahmasmi' self-righteously and becoming one with creation.

The truly awakened has seen a vision of the world which blows his mind – both in terms of the colloquial and the literal meaning of the phrase. He has seen that there is no difference between himself and all he perceives. He also becomes aware of the fact that the reality of all he perceives through his senses is not quite as he perceives it. It is far more 'alive' and luminescent than his senses lead him to believe. It is creative in a manner he could not have even suspected. It is 'full'. The 'void' he had heard about is a myth. Creation is.

Some may see a contradiction here. How can the seer be one with an 'alive' and 'creative' universe? If he is, then there must be a gap between his present state and the state he will be in when something is created further. As such, no person can ever be content. His state will keep changing as the creative universe keeps creating something else. This confusion arises out of the fact that this state of being cannot be expressed in words and conventional meanings tend to confuse the issue. As someone has said, how can one describe what 'light' is to someone who has been blind from birth?

The universe is always in a state of becoming. And, in a sense, so is the enlightened person. However, as he is fully in tune with the universe, he does so effortlessly. This is vastly different from being complacent and not developing at all. Let us never confuse the two. Complacence is truly a world apart from spiritually enlightened contentment.

# In Your Inner Village

## *Embrace Yourself*

Most of us look outside for true peace but this is true only for the peace that we make with ourselves. The consequence of not understanding this is well explained by an African proverb which says, "The child who is not embraced by his village will burn it down to feel its warmth."

This saying, of course, is meant to encourage the villagers to nurture their young ones with sensitivity. However, let us visualize another scenario.

Take a step back and think of yourself as the village child living in your mind. You are surrounded by other villagers. You cannot see them but you can hear what they say.

Do you keep hearing criticism of yourself in your mind? Do you keep hearing voices blaming you for things that happen? Do you keep hearing sentences that say you have this flaw or that and that you are worthless? Do these voices shout, "You are a loser!" at you?

If so, the child that you are is not being embraced by the villagers in your mind. You can be sure such a child will burn the village down one day, just to feel its warmth. What will happen then, you may wonder.

Your inner peace is the first thing such an unembraced child-that-you-are will ignite because this is the most combustible thing in your mental village. The smoke that arises will be made of anxiety, depression, angst and a sense of resignation, loneliness and unhappiness. You may also get physical symptoms, like stomach upsets, heart trouble and, in extreme cases, panic attacks and suicidal thoughts. Sometimes you may smell irrational anger and frustration in this smoke. If unchecked, you will eventually find yourself sifting through the ashes of a life that could have been so much more.

'Embracing yourself' means two things. Firstly, you have to firmly tell these evil villagers, who are busy demeaning you, to shut up. Oh, they will try again and again as they are very persistent but you have to persevere. When negative thoughts about yourself arise, as they will because the wicked villagers do not give up easily, bundle them and imagine them bursting like a cracker. Then watch the pieces float away. If the imagery of explosions does not appeal to you, imagine that thought as a lump of salt, dissolving in water and draining away. Or, use any other imagery that suits you.

If the wicked villagers refuse to shut up despite your best efforts, talk to trusted friends who can help you silence them. Meditation also helps.

Apart from these wicked ones, you also have good villagers in your mind. Embracing yourself means tuning yourself to these good villagers who know you for who you truly are and see the good and lovable in you. When you hear their positive voices in your mind about yourself, hug them and say, yesssss!

Yes, there is a lot of good and lovable in you as it is in almost all of us. The good villagers know these things and keep pointing them out to you, but their voices are soft and get drowned in the hubbub created by the negative ones.

This is not surprising. We are neurologically attuned to pay more attention to negatives than positives. This kryptonite was embedded in our limbic system when our ancestors were living in African forests where a rustle in the bush was more likely to mean a hungry lion than a caring friend. However, we do not live in the forest any more, and have to consciously work towards turning our attention more towards positives than negatives.

It is easy to misunderstand this and carry it to an extreme. Oxygen is essential for our survival but too much of it can kill us. So is self-love. People who overdose on it become egoistic and unworthy. All of us must guard against this.

As the Gita says,

> *uddhared ātmanātmānam nātmānam avasādayet*
> *ātmaiva hyātmano bandhur ātmaiva ripur ātmanah*
>
> Raise yourself by yourself. Do not degrade yourself.
> The self can be the friend of the self and the self can be an enemy of the self.

Be a friend to yourself. Listen to the good villagers in your mind and embrace yourself.

# Dreamwalking

The maker of the universe guards its secrets well. It hides the truth from those who can only see with their eyes, hear with their ears and think with their minds. And so, you have your mathematicians with their complicated calculations, your metaphysicians with their own thoughts, your physicists battering away greater and greater chunks of energy in collisions, all hoping to reach the sanctum sanctorum. You have, too, the religious, with their involved rules and laws, hoping that their leap of faith will land them directly into the chosen goal, never mind that the starting point and the direction of this leap are almost cluelessly chosen.

The eyes, ears and mind are necessary for survival but the maker is beyond the limited concepts accessible to our senses. These can access just one phase out of the almost unlimited possibilities. What then is a person to do? Is all lost as far as the mind is concerned? Is all faith pointless? Perhaps, no.

Remember, the universe exists, and it exists in you. All you have to do to find the truth of the universe is to find the self in yourself. The catch is that you cannot use your mind to find it; at least not your mind in its present frame of reference.

You may have seen 'magic' pictures. In order to make sense of the seemingly repetitive pattern, you have to 'un-focus' your eyes and look beyond the surface of the picture. Only when you do this, does the picture magically appear in three dimensions. However, the moment you try to focus on the print directly, the hidden picture vanishes, leaving the mundane, obfuscating pattern. The universe, as you see it, is in the form of such a magical picture. In order to perceive its true form, you have to un-focus your consciousness to the correct degree and in the right manner. The truth then jumps at you, in multidimensional glory. Not three, not four but many, many more are the dimensions of the universe viewed in this manner, for it straddles many 'phases'. Again, the moment you concentrate your attention on the normally perceived picture, it becomes the day to day, mundane, one you live your life in.

Mystics have realized the above fact for centuries. The un-focussing of consciousness has been tried in a variety of ways. Some have used meditation, others have used drugs. Yet others have practiced physical excess of one type or the other, hoping to overload the mind beyond conventional sanity. It has worked for some and not for others. However, sooner or later, almost all but the real Masters have lost their 'un-focus' and come back to their conventional world, bringing back with them confused pictures for which they had no descriptive words. Their attempts to describe the un-describable has added to the confusion.

Many have dressed up their confusion in magic and myth, and have claimed a monopoly on the truth. And so, myriad religions and cults have been born, with their imagery and rituals, their laws for living and dying, their proscriptions and permissions. A priestly class has sprung up, with priests in assorted headgear talking about their own interpretations. Include in this the hoard of PhDs in mathematics and physics, metaphysics and philosophy. For though they cloak their craft in logic, their class has its own rituals and rules, with about as much chance of finding the ultimate truth as any other 'faith'.

How best to un-focus the mind? It happens in sleep, sometimes, it happens to some of the so-called insane. It happens, too, in some drug-induced trances. However, all these are temporary states, all dream-like and transitory. The 'un-focus' has to be permanent to be of value. This un-focussing must be done while one is conscious and lucid. One can then walk through this dream-like un-focussing, savouring everything and remembering all. This is not impossible. Find a realized Master and he will show you how.

Yes, through the grace of my Guru, I sometimes walk my dreams in other phases. I meet strangeness and familiarity, both with a sense of wonder. I meet others and myself in new circumstances. Some dreams are narrow lanes, dark and forbidding. Others are highways. Yet others are like a winding path through a flower-filled valley. I walk all these like a tourist /observer /student/ adventurer, all rolled in one, in an adventure like none other.

Come, join my seeking and experience for yourself what true wonder can be. Maybe we will surprise each other by meeting ourselves in our selves despite ourselves.

# Mankind's Great Leap of Faith

This note is addressed personally to you. I will not quote Spinoza or Einstein, or Marx or Carl Sagan or anyone else on this topic. What I would like to say is addressed directly to you and needs no endorsement. I only appeal to you to think about this matter dispassionately.

When scientists come across an event that appears to make no sense, they theorise something new and give it properties which would help explain the puzzling phenomenon. Dark matter in the universe, some elementary particles, the position of new black holes and a number of other such things have been originally theorised to explain events which could not otherwise be explained. Scientists then tried to find proof of these formulated things. We, the non-scientists, too, have theorised a force which is perhaps the most powerful one imagined and which helps us make sense of our lives.

We are told that there is a common thread running through the universe. We try to find the common thread running through the farmers committing suicide in our rural areas and a business tycoon's twenty-seven storey residence in Mumbai. We cannot find any. We try to find the common thread in the fact of a European family spending US $350 to 400 on a week's breakfast and a sub-Saharan family spending US $1.35 per week on the same. Again, we cannot find any rational explanation. We try to find a common thread between the look in the eyes of the lamb being sacrificed, and the eyes of the person wielding the knife. We cannot do so.

To resolve this confusion, we have formulated the God-concept. And then, to put the onus on the individual, we have formulated the doctrine of karma, or, to put it in the simplest possible terms, "As you sow, so shall you reap."

The Dalit woman, the dying farmer and the well-housed tycoon are all living in accordance with their past deeds. The higher caste people mistreating the Dalit woman are accumulating their negative karma, or, repaying some old wrong done to them by the poor woman. And God, the divine accountant general, is there to keep accurate records.

The world makes sense once more. There is, after all, justice in the world. The thought consoles us and in our relief, we forget that our belief is merely an unsupported idea.

We have not found any evidence to justify our theory and, not being scientists, we do not even seek any proof. To make our conscience rest easier, we have coined the word, 'faith' and we have appointed keepers of the faith who have ruled, 'Faith needs no proof'. Instead of evidence, we have built a moat in which words like heresy, sin, sacrifice, worship, divine wrath and so on, lurk and make it difficult for the common man to cross. And the seers, who have done so, refuse to divulge what they have found to be the truth. Even Gautam Buddha, when asked about the existence of God, chose to remain silent.

There would be no harm in our artifice but it tends to make us develop a fatalistic attitude and keeps us from making logical deductions. It keeps us from exploring our perplexities, which we have papered over with our un-evidenced theory. Yes, God might actually exist and karma may be a reality; after all we did find evidence of dark matter and we found elementary particles and black holes, too. However, while waiting for proof of God's existence, let us think – what if there is no God and our theorising God's existence is mere self-delusion?

Let us seriously take a few moments and think of this possibility and then view the events around us in this new light. The God-conditioned mind shies away from doing so, but the unaccustomed journey would definitely broaden the mind and, who knows, may lead you to a creation even more wonderful than our limited and limiting views of the creator.

# Is Everything Pre-Ordained?

## *Or How to Interpret the Words of a Seer*

Who am I to argue with my own Guru, Ramana? He did indeed say this:

'Whatever is destined not to happen will not happen, try as you may. Whatever is destined to happen will happen, do what you may to prevent it. This is certain. The best course, therefore, is to remain silent.'

The mistake we commonly make is that we take such quotes literally, without looking at the context. Who did Ramana say this to, why did he say it and what was he really implying? Till I know these things, I will not understand the real meaning of his words.

Taking a saint's words literally can lead to a lot of misunderstanding. For example, Ramana said, 'Be as you are!'

Can a thief say, "Ramana Maharshi said that if you are a thief, be a thief?" Can a cheater justify continued cheating based on this quote? No. The context is important.

I see Ramana's words in the first quote above in the context of the following quote, also by him:

'Engage yourself in the living present. The future will take care of itself. Do not worry about the future.'

The Gita also says the same thing in almost the same words.

Was Ramana trying to advise the seeker that whatever will happen in the future has to happen and you do not spend your time and energy worrying about it? As I was not there and the books do not mention the full context, I can only speculate based on what some other realized seers have said.

On the topic of human will, Paramhansa Yogananda said this: 'If you don't exercise your will power, you will be a weakling, easily influenced by your environment... When you develop will, no matter how you are pounded down by life, you will rise again and say, "I am successful. I can win."'

The *Brihadaranyaka Upanishad* mentions: 'As a person acts, so he becomes in life. Those who do good, become good; those who do harm, become bad. Good deeds make one pure; bad deeds make one impure. You are what your deep, driving desire is. As your desire is, so is your will. As your will is, so is your deed. As your deed is, so is your destiny.'

*Kathopanishad* says, 'He who is ever of unrestrained mind, devoid of true understanding, his sense-desires then become uncontrollable like the wild horses of a charioteer.'

A quote attributed to Lao Tzu says, 'If you do not change direction, you will end up where you are heading.'

There are so many other such quotes from our Upanishads and seers worldwide, pointing to the primacy of one's own actions guided by our will. Many of our texts state that we move up and down on the spiritual ladder by our actions. The whole philosophy of prarabdha is based on the exercise of the human will.

Post facto, we can always say, 'that was written'. However, if we are to mistakenly take Ramana's words literally, it would mean that we need not take any responsibility for our actions. A murderer can say, "That was written. I could not have changed it, so I do not deserve punishment."

The judge would then say, "I condemn you to death. That, too, is 'written'."

If the murderer then kills the judge and that, too, would be 'written' in stone.

Both would be correct, of course, as per the literal interpretation of Ramana's words. But would Ramana have blessed the murderer's conduct and said, "You followed my advice and killed the judge, too? You could not have done anything else. It was written."

If everything is pre-destined, all Krishna had to tell Arjun was, "Do whatever you want." And whatever had to happen would have happened.

As I said, I have no wish to debate this point because all such speculation strengthens the mind and goes against my Guru's core teaching – still the mind.

I recommend that we consider the advice given by seers in light of the context in which they gave it and in keeping with their overall teaching. Such advice should be interpreted by the heart and not by the mind.

# On Happiness

United Nations has declared 20 March as the International Day of Happiness. By itself, this means nothing. One cannot become happy just because of this, as indeed the U.N. World Poetry Day on 21 March will not make one a poet. However, the idea is for us to ignore angst at least for this day and focus on our happiness.

Aristotle said, 'Happiness is the settling of the soul into its most appropriate spot.' When you are asked, "If you could be any three persons, who would you choose to be?" and your answer is: "I, me and myself", you can be sure that your soul has found its niche.

This does not mean that you have to remain exactly as you are. Indeed, that would be passive happiness, eventually leading to stasis and boredom. The urge to be more than you are, to learn new things, to become healthier, to laugh ever louder and more frequently and to make others laugh with you, should remain as strong as ever. However, the critical factor is that this urge should be without goals to be met, without pressure of timelines and without anyone, including you, being judgmental.

This urge, itself, is a source of happiness. It shows you every morning that you are lambently alive, and every night, that you lived in joy.

If you have to 'strive' to be happy, you are not going to find lasting happiness. As Eleanor Roosevelt said, 'Happiness is not a goal... it's a by-product of a life well lived.' To this, I would like to add – and a life being lived well. In a similar vein, Aldous Huxley has noted, 'Happiness is not achieved by the conscious pursuit of happiness; it is generally the by-product of other activities.'

One such activity involves making others happy. As Emerson has observed, 'Happiness is a perfume which we cannot pour on someone without some of it falling on us.'

Achievement, by itself does not result in happiness, particularly if, Alexander-like, we keep being driven to achieve more and more. It is the same with wealth, too. If we never have 'enough' regardless of how many millions we have amassed, wealth may bring comfort but it will not bring happiness.

How, then, can we be happy?

Lucille Ball points out that being able to recognize what makes us happy is a great start. What makes us happy is unique for each of us. For Einstein, it was just 'a table, a chair, a bowl of fruit and a violin'. For Rumi, happiness is when 'we laugh together, you and I/In one form upon this earth, and in another form/in a timeless sweet land.'

Our reason for being happy need not be very elaborate, as Marcus Aurelius points out, 'Very little is needed to make a happy life; it is all within yourself in your way of thinking.' The amazing Helen Keller, happy and successful despite being blind and deaf, agrees and tells us that 'Happiness does not come from without, it comes from within.'

Our seers have also urged us to 'live in the present', 'look inward', 'know thy self', and so on, in our pursuit of spiritual bliss. However, most of us want happiness at a more mundane level. Happiness, for us, is a life free of worries and full of laughter, with joy permeating our lives and of those around us.

Fortunately, as the Dalai Lama has said, your own actions, and reactions, are primarily responsible for your own happiness. The Gita, too, tells us, 'The self is the friend of the self, the self is the enemy of the self'. It is up to you, then. Your happiness depends on you being your friend, not your foe. And a friend of those around you.

Do remember Priyamvada Singh's lines:

*Keejiye izhar-e-mohabbat, chahe jo anjam ho*
*Zindagi mein zindagi jaisa koi to kaam ho!*

Express your love regardless of the consequences
In life, there should be something that emphasizes life!

A final thought: Hafiz said, 'Ever since happiness heard your name, it has been running through the streets trying to find you.'

Today is as good a time to go meet it as any other.

# A Dream Divine

While falling asleep one night recently when I was almost in a meditative trance, Hafiz's lines appeared in my head:

I have learned
So much from God
That I no longer cal myself
A Christian, a Hndu, a muslim, a Buddhist, a Jew

Sometime later at night I found myself in a lucid dream which was the reverse of this sentiment. In it I was a Hindu, a Christian, a Muslim, a Sikh and a Buddhist, all at once. An eminence belonging to each faith asked me questions, and I sensed that only a one-word answer was expected.

The first was a sage-like figure with piercing, all-knowing eyes. The name Yajnavalkya popped into my mind. He looked at me quizzically and said with immense authority, "Have you any idea of the luminescent core of your faith, hiding behind all your rituals and superstitions? Do you think that the almighty divided you in castes and made some of you innately better than others, though the same divine spirit lives in everyone? Have you internalized that the almighty is both male and female and neither? Do you even know the real meaning of the mantras you keep chanting by rote?"

Before I could answer, Jesus appeared, not of the posters but in the image of a middle-eastern man, not too fair, with pronounced Jewish features, vibrant and young, yet looking like compassion personified.

There was sadness in his dark brown eyes and he spoke directly into my heart, "Do you not know that I lived and died fighting the kind of socio-religious bureaucracy my churches have become? Do you think anyone can sell absolution in my name? Do you think that my message is so weak that you have to try to convert others to my path through money, chicanery and downright lies?"

The Muslim me looked up and saw a light – not a dazzling one, but gentle, though bright. From it, a mellow voice asked, "Do you think that your God and mine is so weak that he needs your puny muscles to defend him? Do you think that woman was made less than man and that you will keep her in confinement all her life? Do you not think that our compassionate and merciful God, who you never tire of calling *rahman* and *rahim* – will condone the inflicting of pain and death on others? Do you remember that I have called those worshipping at tombs, fools? Do you think the same God who made you, did not make those who follow a path different from yours?"

I could now see Guru Nanak Dev, too. He did not resemble his usual pictures. He was the young Nanak who gave his money to wandering sadhus. He looked radiant and spoke in gentle yet firm tones. "Did you pay heed when I said, 'As fragrance abides in the flower, as reflection is within the mirror, so does your lord abide within you. Why search for him without?' And, knowing that the same lord abides within each of you, do you get along with each other regardless of *dera*, sect and caste?"

The appearance of a youthful Gautam Buddha made the Buddhist in me quiver with anticipation. However, he looked at me disapprovingly and said, "You claim to be my true follower and sit worshipping my image, but do you not know that I prohibited this during my lifetime and thereafter?"

As these Masters stood in a semi-circle facing me, Lao Tzu unexpectedly materialized in the centre and said, with a wry smile, "If you do not change direction, you may end up where you are heading."

After this, all slowly faded away.

I woke up then, to find that one beam of the early dawn light was shining through the fog on the pine needles on my balcony, making the dew drops on them appear like diamonds. I wondered if it would indeed be a new dawn for me, or if my one-word answer will continue to remain the same.

## The Lonely Sands

One day, as I walked into the desert. Unexpectedly, it spoke to me of love and longing. "I, too, was green, when the cloud loved me," it said, "and now that my beloved has gone, I am arid and brown."

"Together we loved each other for centuries and gave birth to forests where birds chirped and insects skittered. When my cloud went away for good, I hid the bounty we created jointly in my bosom. Over time, it, too, changed form and is now oil, exploited by your kind."

As I sat down on a rock, listening bemused, it continued, "I still wonder why my cloud stopped coming. Did I do something to offend it? Was I not a good mate for it? Did I not raise good forests? Did I not pay obeisance to the wind that brought it here? Such questions haunt me all the time."

"No, I do not think the wind is to blame, though. The cloud has forsaken it, too, because the wind still comes, and it is also hot and dry like me. Together we mourn the loss of what was, and you can hear our moaning among my rocks, sometimes when the wind is feeling particularly sad."

"I know it is the cloud's doing. I hear it is healthy and has moved on to another land, showering its blessings there, making music together with another, as it did with me centuries back."

"That is what happens, child, to all of us over time, when loving stops and the heart dries up. We become arid and feel lost. We even miss the lightning and thunder, which we did not like when we were together. And we start doubting our own worth."

"You are lucky for your lifespan is limited and you can start anew. I will remain like this for eons, dry, over-thinking my loss, living on memories of my cloud, while you dig holes in my heart and take away the only keepsake I have of our time together."

"I have not given up hope," the desert said, "I will wait here till the earth exists. Perhaps, one day, the cloud will ask the wind to bring it here. When it does so, I know the wind will be very happy, too. Together, we will again make rivers here, and trees and birds and insects. I live in hope."

The desert appeared to pause to think and, after a while, said, "Perhaps your race will have passed by then, leaving us in peace again."

The desert was silent after that and I, too, did not know what to say. After a while, as I got up from the rock I was sitting upon, it said, "Goodbye friend, and thank you for stopping by. Come again for I often feel lonely."

I could sense it smile, as it added, "The birds and the insects I had earlier were far better but now I even pine for human company."

## A Prayer

I praise you not, for that would be laughable. Why should I keep telling you childishly how great you are, how powerful, how omniscient and omnipresent? I know that you know yourself while I need yet to know my Self. Such praise would be a waste of time, both yours and mine.

Yes, time may not exist for you but for me in this body-mind, it is of essence, and I want to use it in a more effective way to search for you.

I bribe you not with sundry gifts if 'this' comes true or 'that' for me. I know these offerings mean nothing to you and, to me, these will be a pointless, unworthy distraction. All things belong to you, for you are All-That-Is. What can I bribe you with?

Oh yes, there is one thing that is uniquely mine that I offer to you with all my heart, without any pre-conditions. It is my ego, covering my psyche like Karna's armour, waiting for a Guru to remove it. I wonder if my strong desire to meet you can act as that Guru? If so, my ego is what I offer as my *gurudakshina*. If this strong desire by itself will not suffice, I am sure it will lead me to a Guru who can act on your behalf.

I eschew rituals for I know these are but pointers to the path, however misunderstood they may be, by the naïve. I am on the path and need no directions at this time. I now await the no-door, at which point I will need even the path no more.

I seek you not in trances for the silence of the trance is like suspension of time – a pause button on a video, that starts when the replay starts, at the same place it stopped. Such games are not for me on this quest.

I do not retire to a hermitage for I do not hear the call as yet and those who do so without hearing the call are trying to force something without the universe wishing it. For those like us, our hermitages exist inside our own hearts and there we go whenever we wish.

Yes, instead of all this, I spend my time looking for you. I have an idea what I will find, but knowing and meeting are two different things. One does not taste the fruit by seeing its picture nor does one reach anywhere while poring over the map repeatedly. I know where to look for you and I focus only there.

I seek you not in the hills or plains. I seek you not in shrines or pilgrimages. I know you are closer to me than that. I seek you in the gap between the in-breath and the out-breath. I seek you in the silence between words. I seek you where the musicians singing your praises rest. I seek you all the time, everywhere I am and sound is not. I know that I can hear the divine only when the mundane pauses awhile.

Yes, I am sure that I will find you one day.

And, when I find you, I pray, speak to me like the smile of a child and the look of a seer. Let the joy in your laughter echo silently in my heart. Let me soar on the wings of your blessings, to the land of no-return, and, having been there, come back here humbled, till I am needed no more on this earthly plane. Yes, I can sense your smile, for you know that the land of no return does not mean that there is no return. It only means that the one who returns is not the same as the one who entered it.

I pray, remember my wish when you and I see each other in the mirror of no-mind, which even now waits beyond my senses.

# My Genesis & My Destination

I have discovered inside me an ancient secret which has brought us where we are today. And, knowing the path which we have come by, I know the Tao back. Indeed the journey of self-discovery must start where we came from.

One day, I saw the Tree of Knowledge in the mirror, mocking me. Upside down, its roots my hair, the trunk my spine and the myriad branching webs of my nerves, the arbiters of my senses. And, just then, the stirring of Kundalini at the base of my spine, reminded me of the serpent, coiled, tempting, at the core of this tree, connecting it to the divine. And I knew beyond doubt, my own genesis and my destination.

In the beginning was dust. From this Adamah, Adam, was formed and his spirit included Eve. Indeed, originally, Adam was One, entirely whole, neither man nor woman, yet, spiritually complete and in harmony with all creation, sharing many aspects of the divine.

Then Hawwa appeared, Life, separate, yet wed to Adam and was named Eve. They ate the fruit from the Tree of Knowledge. Having lived with this tree and tasted myself this fruit, I realized that this had to be. With life, ego had arisen, and desire, both enough to undo mankind. The serpent was blamed unfairly, though, indeed, its stirrings could unsettle the unwary.

From this fruit all was learnt. Etz Ha-da'at Tov Va-ra taught Good and Evil, Life and Death, Love and Hate, God and Satan, You and Me, Mine and Thine, Man and Woman, Terefah and Kosher, Nude and Covered, and so, from One, many Twos came to be.

Though it is said, Eve was made from Adam's rib, it was behind it that arose the desire of his heart. If you doubt this, count the twenty-four ribs of your sons and daughters. There are none that are missing in your son.

The Garden of Eden is no garden forsooth as we know such things. It is a blessed continuum where only those can stay, who are One, in tune with it.

Being Two, Adam and Eve were banished from this heaven, but inside them a part of it remained and many centuries later, it passed on to me as my inheritance from the divine. As also, an inheritance from my forebears, the taste of the fruit from the Tree of Knowledge, powerfully colouring all I sense.

From this life and past ones, I know within me, this Pairideiza exists and, one day, I will forget the taste of the fruit and, shunning the Tree of Knowledge, egoless, will return to Edinu where Adam and Eve were once One. I will then be entirely whole, neither man nor woman and yet, spiritually complete and in harmony with all creation.

Then, I can declare that in truth I was always them, and, if I am to believe Ben-Sira, Lilith, too. Older than Eve and Adam's equal, much maligned for refusing to submit. All hiding behind the dream created by the fruit of the Tree of Knowledge that even now resides in me and mediates all I sense.

## If I Could

If I could be all I wanted, what would I be?

Turn by turn I would be so many beautiful and uplifting things.

I would be innocent laughter in an infant and joy in a father. Tenderness in a mother, affection in a grandmother. I'd be the twinkle in the eye of a passionate woman and wetness in a child's kiss.

I'd be eagerness in a lover and rush in desire. I'd be companionship in a couple and freedom in a single person.

I'd be force in storms, fluidity in water, heat in fire, change in seasons. I'd be air on the condor's wing, colour in rainbows, thunder in a cloud. I'd be weight in a snowflake and echo in a bat. I'd be aurora on the poles, the bouquet in wine and the gusto in freshly roasted coffee.

In a ballerina, I'd be grace, and in an athlete, resolve. I'd be nimbleness in a dancer's feet and pure notes in a virtuoso's violin. I'd be taste in my favourite dish, and in cold water for a parched throat, I'd be the relief. I'd be roar in a lion and quicksilver in a cheetah. Yes, and the dance in a peacock and majesty in a Himalayan peak.

I'd be the plot in an engrossing masterpiece and the wit in a classy comedy.

I'd be humility in gurudwara kar-sewaks and courage in the soldiers on the border. I'd be maturity in a sage and light-heartedness in a friend.

I'd be colour in Van Gogh's masterpieces, lilt in beautiful songs and cadence in Sanskrit hymns. I would be peace in sound sleep.

I'd be freshness in the morning and fulfilment in the evening.

I would be fragility in the wings of a butterfly, perfume in rajnigandha, sweetness in honey.

I'd be the aroma in freshly baked bread and lustre in scales of a nimble fish.

I'd be gold in Sun's rays and silver in moonbeams.

And, having experienced these and many more such things, I'd be the calm in a yogi's mind.

What about you?

# Silence Is the Essence

As I sit in my room among the many temples in this holy city, I hear loudspeakers play religious songs so loudly that the whole neighbourhood reverberates. I am dismayed at the ignorance of those who run these temples and at the naivete of the worshippers who think that the louder they play these songs, the more merit they will garner. Do they not realize that the essence of dharma is silence and the louder the faithful get in their worship, the more they alienate their gods? As this thought occurs to me, I am transported back to where I was just a few months ago.

The rays of the morning sun barely penetrated the mist in the valleys and mountains around us. Birdsong softly enriched the atmosphere. In the midst of this awakening, I sat cross-legged, spine straight, facing the Master, awaiting my own awakening.

The Master looked at me and smiled his slight smile. In his eyes I could see the affection in which he held me as, indeed, he held all others, too. He was quiet for a long time and then said, "You are ready. This is your final lesson from me."

I waited, looking at the Master with anticipation. In his silence, I remembered the Master telling us that the beginners recited bhajans. The more advanced chanted mantras aloud and tried to meditate on these. With progress on the path, spoken words became less and less and, eventually, mantras were recited in the mind. After that, even the mantras became silent, and we focused on the inner self, wondering 'Who am I?' Gradually the 'who' went away and only the 'I?' thought remained. I had reached this point. I looked at the Master wondering what came next. The Master had not spoken but in a startled flash I realized what the final lesson was.

The Master's final lesson was just this – *be silent.* Not only in words but also in the deepest stillness of the mind. Even the 'I' thought had to go.

It was as if that the gods were silent when we spoke and they spoke when we were silent. The louder we spoke, the more remote they became and the quieter we became, the closer they came, till, eventually, in the All-Silence, they became us.

With this realization, I looked at the Master's eyes and lost myself in the infinite pools they appeared to be and deeper and deeper my mind drowned. At that moment, I found myself completely lost and completely found.

I felt a gentle touch on my head and the awareness of the world around me returned. I opened my eyes reluctantly to see the Master standing in front of me, blessing me with his palm on my head. I must have lost track of time for it was evening. The birds were silent, and I could see smoke rise from the villages in the valley.

The Master smiled at me and wished me godspeed. He had asked me to leave in the morning for this holy city even though I would have liked to remain there itself; not to be with the Master, for I now knew that he would never be away, but for the tranquility which my body had become used to. However, duty called.

Back in the present, I think of Swami Vivekananda and console myself at the loss of my physical paradise in the hope of the spiritual one. Just then loud music blares from another temple. I shake my head and start walking down for my meeting with the mahants of these temples.

# A Man I Met in Varanasi

I met a man in Varanasi in a narrow lane. Eyes like lamps in the dark, alit in a leonine mane. He sat by the wayside, on the ground reading a holy book. As I passed by, he said something and stopped me with a look.

I stood in silence as he scanned me, up and down. Then he smiled a rueful smile and slowly eased his frown. He spoke, and in his voice I heard the ancients of yore, "You've been called many times but you follow the Path no more! Look inside and you will see, if your actions are just and true. You are here for a purpose. You haven't forgotten, have you?"

He spoke in Sanskrit and, to my surprise I understood all he said. His words echoed loud and clear, inside my heart and head. He went back to his Upanishad, and I was rooted to the spot. Memories came unbeckoned, of what I did and not.

I touched his head; it was a blessing I sought from his matted hair. Waves of love flooded me, ending my despair. Forgetting where I was headed, I turned back from this place. I felt cleansed, awash in amazing grace.

When I woke in my bed, the grace was there to stay. I remembered the old man very well, and what he had to say. I know if I actually went there, I may not find him anymore, but he'll find me when it is time, of that I am sure.

# Common Spiritual Exhortations, Mostly Wasted

We hear many people—especially some publicity seeking Gurus—often repeat stock phrases, which sound good and appear wise to laymen. However, the experienced know that these are merely words and are unlikely to bring true spiritual advancement. This is because we are being told to practice things that are gifts of spiritual advancement, and which cannot be artificially produced through conscious effort by the unripe mind.

This kind of teaching stems from misunderstanding the consequence for the cause, or the destination for the path. We must remember that the state of mind at the beginning of the spiritual path, when a person is merely a *murid* or disciple, is different from how things are when one is inside the door, or even close to it. As the Sufis say, near the door, one achieves the state of *Fana fi Allah,* annihilation in Allah. Zen masters call this state Kensho, an awakening towards one's Buddha-nature. At this stage, this advice, so prematurely prescribed by the well-meaning for the disciple, comes unbidden to the person.

Kensho may come and go, but the next stage, Satori, is permanent.

When a Master enters the door, he is said to achieve *Fana-fi-al baqa* or Satori or Moksha, the irreversible oneness with God. This advice then becomes the permanent norm for the Master. However, as long as we are beginners on the path, we will find it difficult, if not impossible, to implement the teaching in a way which will hasten our advance.

One example of such advice is 'Learn to live in the now'. The past is gone, and the future is yet to be. The present is the specific time you are alive in and you must remain in the here and now. We may focus on the present in moments of tension or great joy. However, focusing on the present all the time is not easy. The very effort to ignore the past and the future detracts from the effort to focus on the present.

This behaviour happens automatically when we have travelled somewhat on the spiritual path and our state of mind has suitably 'matured'. When we are in that state, what we do is not dictated by any consideration other than what we have to do in that moment. The feeling is akin to being on a railroad track, where our course has been laid out for us. The only volition we have is the speed and, that too, is 'suggested' by the prevailing circumstances. We 'know' exactly what has to be done and we do it without a second thought about experiences and about future consequences.

The second example which comes to mind is the exhortation to centre the thought where 'third eye' is said to be, in the middle of the eyebrows. Often this is misunderstood and people try to look at that point, becoming cross-eyed in the process. If this does not happen and one tries to focus the thought at the middle of the eyebrows, one gets so involved in the act of doing so, that the mind refuses to go away, as it should. However, in the state of 'Fana' one just has to sit down to meditate and the whole centre of one's existence can be found to be focused at that point on its own. What one does with it after that, is up to the Guru to advise upon, but the point here is, this is also a post-facto occurrence, not a path to enlightenment.

The third is the advice from well-meaning teachers to repeat Aham Brahmasmi or something similar. Literally, this means, 'I am God'. However, merely repeating this does not make us realize the essence behind this phrase. These remain just words, which, on repetition may produce a hypnotic effect, but will not remove the veil of the mind lying between our body-mind centeredness and our real self. Again, in the state of fana or kensho this happens automatically, and we realize the truth of the phrase Aham Brahmasmi in full measure. We then become one with our divinity. However, till this happens, repeating Aham Brahmasmi may just be passing time verbalizing the unfelt.

Those realized masters who reach the state of Baqa or Satori are permanently guided by their divine selves. It is because of this that Ramana Maharshi said that a realized person cannot commit any sin, regardless of what he does. The universe will not allow the realized person, who is one with it, to commit an act of violation against itself, which is the only definition of sin which the universe recognizes. Till that happens, when we follow the given advice, we confuse the effect for the cause.

It is important to understand the above, because following these well-meant instructions can not only waste a disciple's time, it can also result in frustration at non-advancement on the path.

# A Religion With No Name

Imagine a religion with no name. Imagine a religion that is a framework of feelings not regulations. A religion that is based on how you behave, rather than what you chant. A religion that is a matter of what you give, rather than what you take, a religion of shedding rather than acquiring.

Imagine a religion that focuses on the divine in your heart, not on the name on your lips. A religion that encourages the internalizing this divine, rather than singing its praises repeatedly.

Imagine a religion that tells you to be intrinsically holy, rather than moving you to pen the holy in fences of piety and pent up outrage. A religion that protects mankind instead of a God, who does not need human protection. A religion that finds beauty everywhere and in everyone rather than using 'religious' diktats to selectively mask it. Imagine a religion that promotes joy rather than gravity. A religion that is concerned with the unisex soul, rather than the body you wear this time around. A religion where it matters not whether you are a man or a woman, just that you ARE. A religion that makes you fearless, instead of channelling your life between desire for divine reward, and fear of divine retribution.

Imagine a religion that promotes expansion and makes you see the divine in everything, rather than keeping it in zealously guarded confines. A religion that is inclusive and not limited by labels competing with other labels.

Imagine a religion that does not promise a mythical heaven or hell but encourages you to find peace here itself. A religion that teaches that the divine dwells in silence, and is veiled by loud noises, however 'religious' such noises purport to be. A religion which urges you to realize your real identity, and does not impel you to save someone else's soul without even understanding that there is no one 'else' in the soul's milieu.

Imagine a religion that stills the mind instead of raising it to high pitches of 'religious' or other fervour. Imagine a religion beyond words that divide humans into religious groups, sects and castes.

Imagine a religion that is forward looking, encouraging creativity and learning, rather than enforcing proclamations set in ancient stone. A religion that makes you realize that you are made in the image of God, rather than God being made in the image of you. A religion that impels you to seek the real God-image-you, rather than making you believe that the image you see in the mirror is who you really are.

Often doubts arise as to how you, who are definitely visible, can be made in the image of the divine, who has no shape or form. This doubt curtails your imagination and keeps you in the realm of the gross, confining you to being a man or a woman. It keeps you bound by regulations, rather than the framework of feelings. It makes you cower in fear of God, and those who claim to speak in his name, and propels you into superstitions of one type or another. This fundamental doubt has to go before you can even start calling yourself a seeker.

Imagine a religion that helps you remove this doubt instead of reinforcing it through a web of imagined or prescribed imagery, either concrete or wordy.

I call this imagined religion with no name, 'Spirituality'. It unites as it should, and does not divide as popular religions usually do. When you reach the desired stage, even the framework of feeling dissolves and only bliss remains. Bliss, which the heavens of all religions promise but only after death, from where no one has sent back a message that, indeed, the promise is true.

Finally, this imagined religion with no name will lead you where you and your gods laugh together at how childish you were to think that you were different from each other. Then alone can you see that you are never alone and that you are truly blessed.

# The Truth of My Faith

Are you one of those who wants to learn the truth? Truth about your faith and mine, truth about you and me?

Have you ever sat in silence and wondered about who you really are? After a stage you realize that the name you have called yourself, and others have addressed you by, is just a label, external to you. It really has nothing to do with who you are. It can be removed and yet you remain, in all your humanity. You can remove the layers of the body and the mind and you still remain in your purest form. The name, body and mind are not you.

It is the same with my faith, too. Its label and its body and mind are not what my dharma is. It is beyond this, untarnished with what they have become.

People label my faith by a certain name, the faithful and outsiders alike. They assign symbols, images, rituals and duties to the faith. That is akin to the body. There is a vast store of philosophy in the ancient books. This is the mind of the faith.

Many spend hours talking about these, few really understand and practice the teaching. Once you truly understand the mind of the faith, even that is not needed. Shorn of the label, the body and the mind of my faith, what I have inside me shines in its purest form. I become IT.

However, I live in this world and am accosted on all sides by diverse labels, symbols, images, rituals and duties of different faiths. A body feeding greedily and indiscriminately becomes unhealthy and unwieldy. Similarly, the faith has grown obese, with raucous noises, rowdy festivals, shameless offers to bribe deities, commercial exploitation, politicization and so on. The body of these faiths is in shambles, and those who should be guarding it, are either a party to its deteriorating condition or are too detached and self-centered to be concerned.

The faith has, in many cases, been left to the mercies of sundry people who have no idea of its true form that has sustained it through millennia. They pronounce wrong mantras during havans, but the gullible hear Sanskrit sounding words and are happy. They encourage loudness during worship, aided by amplifiers, without realizing that the essence of the faith lies in silence. They ask for money and gifts in the name of God, and those who can offer more, are accorded a VIP route to the deity. They promote meaningless rituals, the bigger the better. They have made a mockery of the festivals. They embellish idols with gold, when all that these idols want is to be left simple and serene. They dress in gaudy attire and are offended at the drop of a hat, their excuse being that their 'religious feelings have been hurt'. No one bothers to consider if they themselves are hurting the feelings of their religion.

However, there is still hope for my faith. It lies in the many wise seers who still exist. Some of them have guided me to where I am. They are the ones who have realized the truth of what the faith really means. They are one with the universe, the very essence of the faith. In the nature of things, their voice is soft and their teaching silent. Many admire their miracles and even worship them, but very few learn the spiritual treasure they are willing to gift to the sincere learner.

Are you one of these few? Do you want to learn the truth? Are you ready to be really 'faithful'?

# Pillow Talk at the Inn

"Sense my dreams, O soft pillow," I said in the dark, "remember those that leave you mellow or make you chuckle. Pass them on to others who may lay their head on you, in nights to come."

"I will, my dear," the pillow smiled, and asked, "will you do something for me, too?"

"Aye," said I. The pillow whispered, "Respect our room, for it is your haven tonight, and be gentle with our staff. Overlook minor faults. You have borrowed their hands and feet, you don't own them. Like you, they are human, too, and will err sometimes."

It paused and then, sensing my agreement, went on, "Be kind to yourself, also, as you pass, from inn to inn, in your travels."

It must have sensed my surprise, for it continued, "Many come here looking for this and that, almost all, seeking something mundane, something of this world. Very few, like you, come looking for Simurgh."

As I wondered how it knew that I was looking for the divine bird, the pillow smiled, "I can sense your deepest feelings, lying under your dreams," it said. "Finding the enlightened one is a worthy goal, of course, but let me tell you a secret."

A long pause, then, "Travel is restlessness. It leads you away from what you seek, if what you seek is not mundane."

"You are here tonight and will lie in another bed tomorrow, yet you carry inside yourself what you look for here and there. To find that, my dear, unpeel yourself, shed layer by layer, till you reach the core. Shed that, too, till nothing remains. Only then will there be a place for the Simurgh to appear; not before that, however much you seek, wherever you travel."

"You make it sound so simple," said I, "have you met the Simurgh yourself?"

"I am a pillow," it replied, "I have no religion to distract me, no ego to control me and nowhere to go. I find my purpose in giving rest to the restless. I do not have all the baggage you carry, so yes, I have."

"You are here today, someone else will be here tomorrow. In between, I will exist in the stillness. My covers may change and those who use me, but I will remain who I am."

The pillow paused. In the silence I thought of what it had told me. Then, I could sense a smile and the pillow said, "Before I go, let me ask you something. Do you know why the Simurgh jumps into the fire and turns to ash after many years of living a blessed life?"

"No," I admitted, "I don't know."

"I asked the Simurgh this very question, and it told me that, like all creation, the Simurgh too, accumulates some detritus during its long existence. Because of its wisdom, this does not affect its conduct, but it does weigh it down. When the Simurgh feels that it is time to get rid of all this and start afresh, it jumps into the fire and reduces all its accumulated baggage, including its worldly self, to ash."

"But doesn't this extinguish all that it was?" I asked, perplexed.

"The Simurgh itself is beyond its physical self and fire cannot affect it. It rises again, like its brother the Phoenix, and the cycle goes on."

The pillow paused for a long time and I thought it had said all it wanted to. Suddenly it whispered, "The Simurgh's roost, the Tree of Life, is closest inside you, veiled by all that you think you are. Make space for the Simurgh, as I have said, and it will come down from there. You will not find it outside, however many inns you visit."

It waited for me to absorb this and then said, "Now, I will stop talking. You deserve your sleep." I could sense its smile, as it added, "Sweet dreams".

# The Sacred

The sacred is not in the physical presence of holy books. It is in the meaning of the words in them, and in the spirit in which they have been pronounced. Equally, it is in how these words are absorbed and implemented by the seeker.

The sacred is not in the bodies of the teachers. It is in their teaching, imparted either in silence, through a look or a blessing or in words which are understood by the prepared mind. Seers from Buddha to Ramana Maharshi did not like anybody worshipping them. Such worship builds walls between the seeker and the sought, and is counterproductive.

The sacred is not in temples or in shrines. It is in the aura of faith around these shrines, brought there by the original Master and enhanced by the sincere belief of the faithful themselves. Visiting temples and shrines without sensing this aura, sharing it and contributing to it, is a wasted pilgrimage.

The sacred is not in rituals. It is in the faith, sincerity and the understanding with which these rituals are performed. It is better to utilize the time doing something more worthwhile than carrying out a ritual by rote.

Almost all books that are considered holy, contain teachings which, if assimilated in the spirit in which they have been imparted, can bring us closer to the divine. These words are symbols imbued with immense psychic energy.

So are the idols which are worshipped by many. Some teachers have banned the worship of idols. This has been done because they considered idols merely as three-dimensional objects, rather than realizing their true import as charged symbols and gateways, which facilitate access to the divine.

If we are seekers who understand the above, the quantum of the sacred in our books, teachers, temples, shrines and rituals is easy to sense. It is reflected in the deep inner peace we feel after reading our holy books, sitting with our Gurus or worshipping our idols; – or, even just meditating on them. It is also experienced as a sense of oneness with creation and the consequent increase in compassion and empathy. All this is reflected in the extent by which our own thoughts and conduct become more sublime and we become more generous and open-minded.

Then there is the other side of the coin, too, which acts as an easy measure of whether what we are doing on the spiritual path is sacred in the true sense or not. It is this:

If our conduct remains as it was before, if we continue to feel tense or short-tempered, if we persist in behaving inconsiderately and unkindly towards others, if we put our own interest ahead of that of everyone else, and if our greed for money and worldly possessions does not decrease, then all these religious journeys and other practices have not been sacred, as far as we are concerned.

Our efforts have also not touched the sacred, if we remain narrow-minded, if we continue to divide people in categories of those who follow our own chosen religious path and those who do not, and label them as evil or unworthy, or try to convert others through chicanery or bribery to our faith, in the hope of gaining something mundane or earning a place in an imagined heaven.

If any of this happens, we have whiled away precious time under the illusion that we are doing something holy when we are really treating our faith as a trade, in which we think we are doing something for the divine, and then want the divine to do something for us in return, either in this world or the next.

The selflessness of our pursuit, the sincerity of our faith, and the patience and large-heartedness with which this faith is pursued, are of prime importance. These bring out the sacred in ourselves and shows in our conduct.

Therein lies the secret of those seeking spiritual bliss.

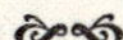

## Laugh, my Love

Laugh, my love, for this life is a comedy though it often wears a sombre mask, sometimes tragic, sometimes farce. See some actors, behaving as if they are kings in truth, and paupers bemoaning their fate for real. All play roles, rosy or grey in a drama directed in such a way, that the audience themselves act the parts so earnestly that they believe with all their hearts that in this fray, they really are who they play.

And the script is a very rough plot to be fleshed out by what the players choose to do.

No one knows what happens when the role ends and the actor moves out of the arena. Where does she go, and what does she do, before re-entering the stage, if at all, in a new act, clad in another costume? Maybe playing a man this time around.

Yes, no one knows where they have been between their shows, though many sell heavenly meadows in a place they haven't seen, whose owner they haven't met, though they claim to be sure, they are his brokers, holy and pure! The gullible pay a commission and buy an 'abode', which the brokers say they will get after the play, and it'll be maintained by the creator, for their pleasure.

It is a measure of the comedic that so many faiths have become multinational organizations, complete with evocative logos, compete around the globe, with the sole purpose of selling their myths to fellow actors through ethical practices which would land them in prison, if they were dealing in anything other than un-real estate, which they do not own, in an imagined land that they have not known, through fancy brochures that they have made, in the roles they have played. Or even entry tickets printed by themselves to take us past an imagined gate, which they have thought up, and none has seen.

Through cleverly crafted incentives and disincentives, they do well and laugh all the way to the bank.

You, too, laugh my love at what we believe to be true, for it is a comedy of epic proportions.

Only some witnesses, knowing this, are at peace. Dotted here and there in time and space, they can be seen hallowed with amazing grace. And looking at them, we know that they have been where they cannot be seen by other actors, regardless of what the self-appointed brokers may say.

These seers true, are the only ones worth listening to. They claim no ownership, and sell nothing to me and you.

Till you are one such, laugh my love, like an infant, just arrived on this earth who knows nothing of this play. Who knows not, how to atone, how to pray, what 'sin' is, what it's not. One who is too new to have forgot who sent him here.

Yes, laugh my love, laugh and play the role you have, the best you may, and remember, whatever you do on this stage, there is no cause to look for applause from where you came, regardless of what some brokers may claim.

You are the actor, you are the audience and, strange as it may sound, on this play-ground, it is you, who are your own critic, too.

# My Spiritual Journey

Early on, I told myself that I could see further if I stood on the shoulders of giants. However, the real ego-driven reason for climbing up there was that I wanted other people to see me better.

Soon I found that my vision was impaired and my words derivative. I spoke, not with understanding, but by rote. My convictions, like my feet, were not rooted in the ground but dangled in thin air.

I looked around from up there and saw a number of poseurs like me, some of them richly caparisoned, donning masks of faux wisdom, preaching with borrowed words. Listening to them I realized that I was trivializing my own worth. Perhaps the wisdom of the giants had some effect on me. Even high up, I felt small. I realized my folly, and climbed down, back to earth where I belonged.

I felt puny, and then, like the child I was spiritually, I stood in the shadow of these masters, holding the finger of one or the other. There were so many – Shirdi Sai, Ramana, Nisargadutta, Papaji, Rabiya al Adawiyya, Mansour al Hallaj, Rumi, Gibran, Angelus Silesius, and many others. It mattered not who I was with at any time, for all of them were, in essence, the same.

I grew under their care, slowly but surely, by letting their wisdom permeate my innermost depths, nurturing the spiritual me. Forgetting most of what I thought was real was the most difficult, but in their words, and in their silence, I realized that it was indeed a simple quest and not as complex as many interpreters of 'holy' texts made it out to be.

I also found that, shorn of the aura of 'holiness' the ancient texts were nectar that could help me grow. These, too, nurtured my roots, and the sapling that I was, flourished.

Patience and faith became my truth, and I watched 'me' fade into 'us' and then, at least for a few magical moments, at times, into nothing or into all. In these rare moments, I view existence almost from the same perspective as these Masters. I look into their eyes and feel them smiling at me, encouraging me on my quest, with their smiles of belonging and affection, a Master's gift to a sincere novice.

When these moments fade away, as they always do, I do not find myself a small child any more, clutching the fingers of any of the giants like someone who wants to be 'saved' from the cataract of emotions. The flood has abated, and though I am not as tall as the giants, I am able to sense something of their grace in myself, telling me how to get where they are. The rest is now up to me.

Do I feel pride at how I have grown? Does a sapling feel proud that it has become a young tree? That in me, which felt this pride when I first climbed on their shoulders, now lies discarded in the trash bin of other abandoned stuff. Or, at least most of it is there. Some still persists, but I now know what it is, and how to keep it in its place. When that also goes, I will belong to the assembly of giants, as one of them – nay, as them, for good.

That day is still far in time, but in sight now. I look forward to reaching there, not with hope or elation or a sense of achievement, but with quiet equanimity. I know what I will find there, for, off and on, I have been in that continuum. To be there permanently, it is critical that the desire for that bliss and the expectation for it must go away, as must all other desires and expectations.

As these Masters have emphasised, I AM THAT. Under their benign guidance, first THAT vanished, then AM. Now I get a glimpse of the possible, but the 'I' still holds me back. When the 'I' also vanishes,

I will be one with what is not lost, the real ME that hides behind this mundane 'I'.

The sapling has become a tree and is growing gradually taller. One day the canopy will reach where the sun shines without any shadows. There is no urgency. I will reach there when I do.

I have written this down, not to announce where I am on my spiritual path. I have done this because I know that many of my readers are on this path, and some may find a kindred spirit in me, through these words.

# The Tomato As a Teacher

The tomato plant belongs to the deadly nightshade family, Solanaceae. Its flower, stem and leaves are reputed to be poisonous. Yet we eat the tomato without any ill effects. This has two important lessons for us.

*The first lesson is that we must live in the present, free of the baggage of the past.* Most of us routinely live in the cognitive past, often without realizing it. In our current social discourse, I find a number of cases where someone has mentioned that a person or an organization is evil because of an action that took place several decades ago.

We think that what they were as flowers, they remain as fruits. While some people and organizations continue to be a reflection of their past selves, many others do evolve into more benign avatars. However, our views seldom change, especially when motivated people keep hammering at real or imagined sins committed in the distant past. This is ably abetted by reports which focus more on sensationalism than on substance.

This typecasting happens in families, too. So many families live in an environment of bitterness because one member keeps dwelling on mistreatment in the distant past by a relative. He refuses to consider that the relative they blame may have evolved for the better. Another example is this. A daughter-in-law remembers being 'mistreated' by a mother-in-law when she was a new bride some fifty years back. Now her mother-in-law is in her eighties and has perhaps evolved into a wiser person, calmer and benign. However, the daughter-in-law continues to see her as evil. This affects everyone in the family and much angst is caused by the habit of continuing to see only the poisonous flower, even though it has now been transformed to an edible fruit.

This affects the next generation as well. Fed on bitter family history, coloured by emotional perception, children get alienated and acerbic. They, who never saw the original flower, picture the fruit as being of a similar nature, and this distorts their entire perspective. Such living in the past can make the present hell, not only for the perpetrator concerned but also for all those around him.

The second lesson is even more important. *We must not believe everything we read or hear.*

Though tomatoes belong to the nightshade family, the alkaloid they produce is tomatine, which is a relatively benign glycoalkaloid. It is not very toxic and one has to ingest really large quantities of the leaves or flowers to get ill. After laboratory tests, consuming tomato leaves has not been found to be adverse to human health. No wonder, in countries where this myth still has to take hold, tomato leaves are eaten without a problem.

India's current public discourse is largely based on believing whatever people see on the television or read in newspapers, magazines or on social media. Most people have exploited this and proved Goebbels right. He said, 'It would not be impossible to prove with sufficient repetition and a psychological understanding of the people concerned that a square is in fact a circle. They are mere words, and words can be moulded until they clothe ideas and disguise.'

Exploiting the above, our current society is being presented constantly by some motivated people as being poisonous, based on a few venomous incidents. These are repeated ad nauseam and people start believing that India is filled with a poisonous miasma. As Goebbels also pointed out, 'the media can be played like a keyboard.'

We do not have to keep living in the past or believe everything we read or hear. These are conscious choices and our experience with the tomato plant should definitely teach us to make the right choice – an informed choice.

ঌ৵

# Conceptions

## *How We View God*

Some people think God is a gardener and they are flowers in his garden. They wait to be cut and put in the divine vase up above. For them, there is no need to do anything as their fate is in the hands of their caretaker. These people are fatalists who have surrendered their right to free action, either through ignorance or laziness.

Some people think that God is a restaurant manager and they are guests in the divine café. They expect their needs to be catered immediately and get annoyed if divine assistance does not follow their raised finger. These are the perpetually dissatisfied.

Some think God is a rather frightening father figure, easy to annoy and petty enough to demand grovelling self-abasement from his children as his rightful due. Such people crawl through life without the spiritual self-respect which is their right as human-born.

Some think God is either a sadistic sovereign or a witch-doctor and they are his subjects. He demands his dues through bizarre rituals and painful asceticism. These are the egoists who negate whatever little worth there may be in their efforts, through pride in their physical excesses. They despoil their physical selves, the safeguarding of which is their first duty.

For some, God is a cave where they can take shelter from the storms of life. They have surrendered their courage and go about discontented if an occasional shower strikes them, without realizing that their cave may be a creation of their own minds and without knowing that circumstances lack their imagination.

For many others God is a cause. Their religion boils down to fighting others for slights they imagine having been inflicted on their God by others whose idea of God may differ from theirs. Their God is not a spiritual one, it is just an excuse to give vent to their violent inner selves. They are grievance collectors, and attract others like themselves is an unholy dance of acrimony and death. Such people go through life with a self-righteous smirk, protecting an idea of an idea, the original of which they have no idea of.

If one were to view God beyond a universal cosmic presence, though there is no compelling need to do so, God can best be visualised in all that is good in us. No amount of external rituals can help if we do not heed the God thus defined. On the other hand, no 'transgressions' worthy of fear will arise if we heed this God. And the best worship will be to implement the gentle advice of the goodness in us, advice which is so often drowned in the clamour of church and temple bells, or the loudness of the muezzin's call.

# Extremes of the Spiritual Quest

## *A Warning for the Impressionable*

We often come across people who inflict pain on themselves by poking their tongues with small spears, or standing on one foot for days or months. Some people resort to extreme rituals in burning ghats, or severe fasting. Some others use hypnotic drugs. Unfortunately, some new seekers find these practices fascinating, and end up in the hands of these ersatz gurus whose efforts misdirect them onto another path altogether.

Those unfamiliar with the subject often wonder at the connection between such extreme practices and the spiritual quest. There is a connection, but this is like the connection between an object and its distorted reflection in a flawed mirror. The reflection is neither the original, nor true to it. However, by the time the misguided seeker realizes this, he is trapped in a state where he is beyond realizing anything much.

All these practices arise out of a desire to seek a short-cut to spiritual enlightenment. Their practitioners have learnt that the influence of the mind has to be removed completely if enlightenment is to be achieved. These practices are their effort to strain the mind so much that it snaps its links with reality. The resulting stage is a temporary suspension of the world and a trance-like effect, where an alternate reality takes hold of the mind. Such people mistake this as a sign of spiritual advancement. However, their quest takes them on a path which degrades their physical health and distorts their mental well-being. No spiritual good comes out of this, though sometimes the practitioner tends to achieve certain siddha powers, which, in turn feed the ego, and make the spiritual quest even more difficult.

It is true that for spiritual enlightenment to happen, the mind has to be suspended, and an alternate reality accessed. In the spiritually enlightened, this is a benign alternate reality where duality gives way to the feeling of oneness with everything in the cosmos. The hallmark of this is benevolence and bliss, which the Sufis have called Baqa or, if it is temporary, Fana. Zen masters call this awakening Kensho or Satori.

This comes through gradual practice of meditation with proper focus which results in a steady advancement on the path. It can also come through the entire submission to a higher power, like Mirabai or Rabiya al Adawiyya did. This is not easy to achieve.

Nisargadutta Maharaj has equated this with the ripening of the fruit, which, when fully ripe, falls on its own and cannot be put back. Some seers like Ramana Maharshi have achieved this spontaneously. Obviously, the fruit was ripe in his case to start with.

An artificial effort to force the fruit to ripen by putting it in a pressure cooker only cooks it and it emerges in another form altogether which is very different from a naturally ripened fruit. All those who practice extreme disciplines like torturing themselves or taking drugs or practicing horrific rituals in burning ghats, similarly cook their minds into a state which may make it feel like it is ripe for enlightenment, but which converts it to a state where its very fabric is destroyed.

It is for this reason the realized Masters never advocate such extreme practices for their disciples. What distinguishes such Masters is that their presence is comforting and their grace is gentle. Yes, they may set difficult tasks for some disciples who they think need more discipline but these tasks are only meant to remove the kinks in the disciple's mind and not to pressure-cook it. They let the fruit ripen on the branch and only help by providing the correct nourishment and atmosphere for the disciple. This company of good men, satsang, is conducive to this process and is valued in spiritual and social texts.

The other kind of 'gurus'—those who use sex and/or drugs and offer to 'help' disciples achieve their goal—demonstrate a lot more pyrotechnics. They worry about looking the part, and they never appear benign. However, their spiel is beguiling, and it is very easy for the eager, half-informed, spiritual seeker to be taken up by such tantriks and faux gurus.

If such a guru is a siddha with even minor powers, the trap becomes more honey-laced. However, we must educate our young in the proper context of these so-called gurus and explain that there are no short-cuts to spiritual bliss. Such ersatz gurus merely misguide and never achieve spiritual bliss themselves, despite all the song and dance.

It is essential to see these practitioners of the extreme for what they are – posturing professionals, who are misguided themselves and will lead whoever falls within their sphere of influence far away from the goal.

## The Five Metamorphoses

In explaining spiritual advancement in *Thus Spake Zarathustra,* Nietzsche says, 'Three metamorphoses of the spirit I designate to you: how the spirit becomes a Camel, the Camel a Lion, and the Lion, a Child.'

We behave like camels when we take over burdens of the world. Then we need to evolve into a lion because the lion can do many things that the camel cannot. The most difficult of these is 'to assume the ride to new values' – from the YOU SHALL of conventional religion to the I WILL of the more enlightened.

The third metamorphosis is to a child. According to Nietzsche, 'the child is innocence and forgetfulness, a new beginning, a game, a self-rolling wheel, a first movement, a holy Yea.'

More realistically, a person goes through five metamorphoses, not three. The first is when a man starts out as a rat – ever greedy, gnawing at everything even when not hungry.

The second is the camel. According to Nietzsche, we become camels in order to satisfy our ego. I feel our motivation is our compassion and love and, to some extent, social compulsions.

The third is the lion, where the desire to break out free and act is foremost. Courage is the hallmark of this stage. 'You Shall' is a powerful highway and paths diverting from it are seeded with the thorns of blasphemy. Most people find the mountain of blasphemy too difficult to cross and without crossing it there is no entrance to the fertile valley of 'I Will'. The lion is needed for this.

The fourth is the elephant, where man acquires dignity and wisdom and the aggression of the lion is mellowed. The Ganesh image symbolizes this. Wisdom and maturity are must before they, too, are subsumed in innocence.

The fifth is the child where innocence is the prime quality. Eashoa', who most know as Jesus, also mentions this. When his disciples asked, "On what day will you be revealed to us, and on what day shall we see you?" Eashoa' said: "When you unclothe yourselves and are not ashamed, and take your garments and lay them beneath your feet like the little children and trample on them, then [you will see] the Son of the Living One, and you will have no more fear."*

Most of us are stuck in the 'rat' stage – our quest for food, clothing and shelter guide us throughout our lives, as does our greed for acquiring more and more.

Another big challenge is to move from the camel to the lion stage. We are so conditioned by our education, our traditions and our social mores that few can break out of the mould of 'You Shall' and strike out on their own path of 'I will'.

Moving on to the elephant stage is essentially a function of killing the ego. For some, this comes naturally and for others through the guidance of a Master. In most, regrettably, this never happens.

From elephant to child is easier as wisdom is already there to guide us. The fruit is ripening and will fall one day.

Ramana Maharshi has shown how to overcome inter-stage resistance. Papaji quotes this from his meeting with Ramana:

I asked, "Bhagavan, I have been an ardent devotee of Krishna, but now I can't say his name anymore. What is happening?"

"How did you come here?" he asked.

"By train."

---

* Gnostic Gospel of Thomas [37]

"Where is the train now?"

"The train was at the station and now it has gone."

"And from the station to the ashram?"

"From there I took a bullock cart to you. I sent the cart away once I got to the ashram."

Bhagawan Ramana said, "You made use of the train, but then you left it behind. Then you took a cart and also left it behind when you arrived to see me because it was of no further use. Like this, all the things you performed are of no use now and they will be left behind. It is most important that you keep your intention in mind. You wanted to see me and now you are here only because you left the train and cart behind."

Seekers should introspect and determine which stage they are in and how they can move forward. If needed, an able Master should be consulted.

# On the Ides of March, and a Wish for my Antony

"The evil that men do lives after them, the good is oft interred with their bones."* So said Marcus Antonious. No Caesar am I, and when I'm past the gate, may my fate dictate things the other way round.

May the evil I've done burn on my pyre and the good escape the fire, to live on in these children and theirs, my own and others, who I cared for much, and whose lives my good fortune made me touch.

When they cried, unlike Caesar, I wept not, but helped wipe their tears. When they shivered, I often calmed their fears. I tried to be there for everyone, and I did what I could, harming none. When I pass on, I daresay, my real work would have just begun.

May they remember me with a smile when they tarry awhile and look back at these times. May they feel they've done their best, when their bell chimes, not only for themselves but for all they met, and made the world a tad better.

Then there is what I write. For the earnest seeker may my poems and prose serve as a guide. May these not be a waste of ink. And my stories – may they amuse the readers and make some think.

I'm not perfect but won't excuse myself by saying 'no one is'. I'm not perfect because of my own character flaws, and I know this. Yet, may the evil I did be forgot, and the good live on generation after generation, for my loved ones, and for my nation.

---

* Shakespeare, William. *Julius Caesar*

And, then, if an Antony or Antonia were to orate for me; unlike Mark, let them not say that their heart lies with me on my pyre. Let them say, His heart beats in me, and sets my spirits afire!"

I would then have been worthy of this birth.

# I am Akshara

I was born of the omnipresent Aum, as the divine alphabet. Whether I arrange this as a scripture with my life or a pedestrian book is up to me.

Inside me, I realize why the ancients called the Word, 'A-kshara'—the imperishable, that which cannot be destroyed, the font of knowledge—for, at my core, that is my reality too.

Let me not debase it by smudging my story with pettiness, unkindness or any such act. Let me not fling the sacred-in-me here and there in unworthy fits of rage. Let me not break the nib of my pen because I find someone else has a better one. Let me not get carried away by power or fame, or by dismay and hopelessness, all of which are like the transitory shadow of clouds passing over the unblemished Word.

Let me remember that my nature is Light. That is what I was born to describe, and that is what I should strive to be through what I do.

Let me remember...

# All-That-Is

We are stardust, you and I, but it doesn't matter, 'Our atoms are starburst born' is just idle chatter. We don't have to look too far to know who we really are. We are the Self that brings to life dead atoms from a star.

We were here when the stars were born. We watched the universe alight, and we waited till it was ready, to give our imagination flight, then we took this and that, and fashioned the body-mind you see. We entered and gave these life, that's who we are – you and me.

The time will come one day, when we will end our stay. Dust shall return to dust, and you and I will go away, to plan another play on earth, or at another place, to amuse ourselves and to learn, till our final grace.

Then return to our mother-form, waiting for us all the while, watching the stars whirl around, with a knowing, indulgent smile. Universes will come and go, made how we choose our play, our Life Force is All-That-Is, in different forms, having its say.

# Arguments at the Fish Shop

## *Of Samaq and Matsya, Maach, Poisson, Psari, Pesce, Yu, Sakana, Ryba and Dag, too*

The old man saw Rama and Abdullah arguing outside the fish shop. He was widely respected in the village, and as he neared, both greeted him. He asked them why they were arguing and if he could help resolve the problem.

Rama said, "He says that I am offending him because I do not come here to purchase samaq."

Abdullah responded angrily, "Samaq is the only thing worth buying. This man is doing things against our belief."

"What have you come to buy?" the wise man asked Rama.

"I have come to get some matsya," he replied.

"Aah, I see the problem," the wise man said. Just then he saw his Italian friend pass by. He stopped Luigi and asked, "Luigi, why have you come to this shop?"

Luigi replied, "*Sono venuto a comprare il pesce, ovviamente.*" I have come to buy pesce, of course.

"*Non, non, il n'y a pas de pesce ici, je ne vois que du poisson!*" Jules, who had stopped too, said, "No, no, there is no pesce here, I can only see poisson!"

The old man laughed and said, "I see that people come to this market to buy matsya, samaq and pesce. I am from Tibet, and I have come to buy nyi tro. There are others here bargaining for maach, psari, yu, sakana, ryba and so on.

He paused and then said, "Look at what is being sold in the market. Is it different for different customers or are they all buying the same thing?"

"There's only matsya here," Rama said.

"No, there's only samaq here," Abdullah said.

"What nonsense!" Luigi replied. "All I can see is pesce."

"Stop this!" Jules said, "Are you all blind? Such wonderful poisson is here, and you all can't see it!"

Benjamin, who had paused to listen to the discussion, piped in, "I do not understand you people. The only thing available here is dag. There is nothing else in this shop."

"Can't you see that all of you are calling the same thing by different names?" the wise man asked.

"That may be so," Abdullah replied. "But Rama and Luigi and Jules and Benjamin, all have their own recipe books and even cook it differently. If they had any sense, they would call it samaq, and follow our recipe book."

"I see," said the wise man, "but is that enough reason to fight?"

"We have been told to make everyone call this samaq, and make them follow our recipe book. I must insist on this. If they do not do so, I will consider them my enemies."

"You are crazy," Luigi replied, "you better start calling it pesce, and cooking it in our way, otherwise things will not go well for you."

At this, Abdullah started turning red with anger.

"I do not have time for this just now," the old man replied. "I will now go and buy my nyi tro. My recipe book is waiting at home, and I will cook according to what it says, because that is what I like. In the meantime, all of you just think about whether names and ways of cooking the fish are more important than the attention you pay while purchasing the fish."

Saying this, he walked away towards the fish shop. Rama, Abdullah, Luigi, Jules and Benjamin remained where they were, each insisting on acceptance of his own name and his way of cooking the fish, as per his own revered recipe book.

All the while, the fishmonger waited patiently, smiling and shaking his head.

# Me the Sakadagamini

Various cultures have different names for stages on the path. These labels do not matter. The number of stages also varies—from four to eight—but these numbers do not matter either. These are merely useful crutches to explain the unexplainable experience to questing minds.

Here are the four stages from Theravada Buddhism from my own perspective.

When Sotapanna I was, entering the stream, I often had this dream.
That who I think, isn't who I am – I'm neither a 'Sir', nor a 'Ma'am'.
I waded in, and once in a while, what I saw made me smile
With faith and patience I entered a world, where I found the self unfurled.

But back on the shore I return, a Sakadagami, scared of the true.
It's unsettling to learn, who you think, isn't entirely you.
The 'obvious' is a temporary one, it's but a part of the whole,
Come here to live and learn, just an actor playing a role.

Anagami I'll be, maybe one day, when I can turn the page,
It'll take courage, 'n blessings divine, to exit this fanciful stage.
Then I won't return but yet be here, till this body lets me be,
There's little that'll change my dear, in me that you can see.

Sakadagami I am, I can't unsee, who I saw as the uber-Me,
In calm moments I often find, an urge at the back of my mind.
To go back there and remain, just the witness of this play
An Anagami, calm and wise, patiently waiting for the day.

When the divine will descend and make sure
That I become an Arahant, to birth no more
But I strive not, for all striving is by my mind
And that's one thing that I must leave behind.

In my heart I really know
I have a very long way to go
But in utter silence, I heard a whisper say
"Have faith and stay still, you'll be there one day."

So I wait patiently and bide my time
Till I taste the sublime.

# The Fate of a Religion

The Master was feeling his age today. His joints ached and there was a slight wheeze in his breath. Yes, he mused, they said he was a great man, the Master of Masters, but in the physical context, he was just a man. His body, too, will age and die like the prophets of old, like so many of his friends, like his beloved wife and like most of his enemies. The cycle of life and death must continue. He felt that the time was near when his role on this plane would end.

He did not fear death. Far from it. He welcomed it as an omen of peace and harmony; as a sign of continuity. He knew that it was just a transition. 'He' could not die. It was just his body that would perish. After that, new adventures awaited.

He had already told those who called themselves his followers not to mourn his passing. He had lived a full life and now it was time to go. And what a life it had been!

The Master smiled at his memories and picked up a book bound in gold thread. It was his life story, they said. He opened it at random, then smiled again. They had written down the words but the spirit, the essence of what he was, did not exist in this book. The messenger appeared to have overtaken the message. So it had been for all conventional religions and, sadly, so was the fate of his teaching, too.

The Golden Book reminded him of a recipe which listed the ingredients and mentioned how they should be mixed and processed, but did not give the taste or nourishment which only eating the food could provide. Yes, that was perhaps what this book about his life resembled. Perhaps even worse; perhaps just a menu card in a fancy covering. Surely with the gold binding and cover, it must belong to an expensive inn! He laughed out aloud, startling the girl putting water by his side. Whatever possessed his followers to glorify him thus? Why should they think that binding his life-story in expensive covers would make it any richer? If it was not rich to start with, you could inlay it with diamonds and it would not improve. And, if it was innately rich, even a simple paper cover would have sufficed – nay, perhaps would have improved the value of the contents.

He had never understood this desire of people to embellish everything in what they thought was rich and gorgeous. Today they were doing it to his life-story. After he died, they would probably gold-plate every word he had said and embalm his memory in amber and myrrh. They had done it to all other such books in the past. He wondered how his words would be able to live, then. Did these people not understand that words and deeds were also alive, that they had a vitality of their own, which suffocates and dies when they are idolised? Words need to be used as living things, not as holy symbols.

Perceiving where things were headed, the Master realized that too much reverence was as bad, perhaps worse, than too little reverence, as far as understanding something was concerned. Too much reverence set the object of reverence far apart from oneself, and one could not truly understand something spiritual if it was so separated. In order to understand, the thing had to become a part of oneself. The food had to be eaten to be known. The path had to be travelled to experience new places. Gilding the recipe book or worshipping the road sign would not lead anyone to the promised nectar or the Father's Kingdom. Too much reverence made it remain at the altar, unreachable and impossible to know. It killed all independent thought for to question became heresy.

He had visited some houses where the so-called 'faithful' gathered for their ritual prayers. They called these 'Ga'ms' and were called Ga'mis themselves. Ga'ms were always made facing the direction of the Master's hometown, and, in his hometown, facing the direction of his home. The book of his life story, including his teachings, called the 'Word', was kept on a platform and covered with an ornate cloth. One or more people were always in attendance, near the platform with a flywhisk waving away imaginary flies in the air-conditioned ambience. No one was allowed to keep the 'Golden Word' on the floor or to handle it disrespectfully, or to make a notation on it, even if it was just a copy or a translation. It appeared that it had become more important to revere it than to follow its spirit. He sometimes shuddered that his words had been reduced to icons so early. He feared that soon, people will just keep reciting them by rote without understanding anything.

He had another concern. Throughout history he had seen people exploit myths and icons for their own purposes. Some dressed up in robes and complicated, majestic-looking headgear, surrounded the faithful in complicated rituals and called themselves 'the chosen ones'. They accumulated tremendous wealth, some of it even by dispensing seats in heaven to the 'sinners' in return for money, gold or land. The myth of their Master had served them well. Others made a show of asceticism and kept their beard and hair in a certain way and identified themselves as the guardians of the truth. Sometimes they took pride in wearing short dresses so that their arms and ankles showed, marking them out as extra-faithful. Egoistically, they revelled in power over laymen and, more so, over lay-women. Yet others went about unkempt, with long matted hair, from pilgrimage to pilgrimage and thought they were doing the divine one's bidding. Then there were those who flagellated themselves and thought this will bring them special favour from the father-in-heaven.

He feared that his followers, too, will become like this, fighting with others and with each other, divided into numerous sects, closed-mindedly interpreting his teachings, thinking them the ultimate Word, on pronouncing which all thought ceases. He feared that their brains would get fossilized and they would stop thinking for themselves. He wondered what would have happened to him had he done that. From the very beginning of his life, he had had to think for himself and often this thinking was against the popular norm.

He thought of the time when he was born – the son of a king who had recently died, quietly whisked away at birth to avoid being killed by his uncle, the regent. Raised as a shepherd, he was imprisoned and given the death sentence by a governor appointed by his uncle. Buried alive, he had managed to escape with the help of his faithful family nursemaid – 'arisen' was the word his followers used with awe. He had finally won his kingdom back, but not before he fought and killed the island despot who had kidnapped his wife. Then seeing the futility of war, he had left his kingdom and donned a monk's robes, meditating in the forest and gaining amazing insights into his real self. Out of these had come wisdom and, to his surprise, words from nowhere, which he heard aloud in his mind. When he recited these, at first people thought that he had gone mad, but then they took these down and revered them as the word of God.

Yes, indeed. What would have happened if he had only done what the prevailing wisdom dictated – cow-towed to his uncle, perhaps, and lived a luxurious and sterile life, ruling a kingdom under his uncle's thumb. That was, of course, if he had not been killed first.

He had not volunteered to become a messenger of God or of anyone else. Things had happened in his life for which he could best describe himself as a witness and a vehicle. He felt the same as other men. He did not feel any 'holiness' in himself. Yet, despite his expressly banning any form of worship of himself or, indeed of any idols or books, this was slowly coming to pass. He had heard of his toe-nail cuttings being sold by the servant-girls and installed in shrines as holy relics. The hair from his head and beard were considered the property of the barber, till he asked the barber to leave every single cut strand in the room. He wondered what would happen to his body when he died.

In this mood, he suddenly felt one of his trances coming on and the voice, which had spoken inside him so often, said gently, "The time is now. Go!"

The Master heard and understood. He got up slowly, looked back at his room with bemusement and went out into the dusk. His faithful servant, who was waiting outside, tried to follow him, but, after being assisted on his horse, the Master dismissed him. When the servant asked when the Master would be back, he just gave an enigmatic smile, blessed the servant and willed his horse to move. Responsive to his slightest thought as usual, the handsome animal started moving towards the forest with an unhurried but firm gait.

He had chosen the time carefully. Most of the town-folk had gathered in their Ga'ms at this time for the evening worship and there was hardly anyone on the streets except some children who he waved a cheery goodbye to. They responded in kind. Some adults bowed to him as he rode – he raised his hand in a blessing to them.

He rode out to the forest surrounding the town. He knew this forest well; he had often visited it and sat in hidden caves in silent meditation for hours. After riding on narrow, winding paths, he reached the fork near the tree under which he was supposed to have gained his wisdom. He bypassed it by taking the left path, to avoid the constant presence of the priests and acolytes there. He smiled to himself – why did they think that there was something special about this tree? It was like most other trees, with roots, bark, branches and leaves. All the trees spoke to him of peace and harmony, but never as teachers. If trees had the power to endow wisdom, all the forests would be full of wise monkeys and lions. He shrugged and quietly rode inside the darkening forest.

After crossing a shallow stream, he dismounted and silently commanded his horse to go home. The horse hesitated, looked at him for a moment and then obeyed. Indeed, it seemed to the Master that it was so easy to communicate with animals. Monkeys became quiet in his presence. Dogs sat down at his feet even if he just thought that it would be nice if they would do so. Birds would come and cluster around him and peacocks would dance if he just smiled at them. When one merged with nature, nature welcomed one with open arms and all its creatures became friends who understood you. Except man, the Master thought, ruefully. Man, it seems, is the most unnatural of animals and the farthest from the purity embodied in nature.

The Master followed the horse till it had turned on the path and was out of sight. Then he walked slowly through the dense forest for about five minutes. His special cave was here, its mouth obscured by the branches of a large bush. He entered it and lit the small lamp, which he had kept there. Then he sat down on the jute rug and tugged at a rope he had strategically arranged months earlier. A large boulder rumbled down the entrance and was followed by a minor landslide, covering the entrance. The flame of the lamp moved and so did his shadow on the wall. The Master smiled to himself – his vanishing would be one more mystery in a life full of mysteries. He then went into his last meditative trance. The lamp, too, flickered off after some time.

And then…

He knew Masters like him never really died. In fact, no one did. They just cast off their bodies and became free. This freedom was relative, of course. Some just became free to rue their lives and then to experiment with more. Some, like the Master, became free to do as they pleased.

The concept of time had changed for him. Time, he knew, was a construct of the mind and had vanished when the mind went, along with the body. The Master found himself able to visit anywhere he wished at whatever time period he wanted to see.

The first timeframe he decided to explore was the immediate aftermath of his vanishing. He did not want to hear lamentations at his going away, so he chose a time about two months after his death. He found that there was a widespread belief that his horse had carried him to heaven and then had been sent back. There were temples in which idols of the horse were worshipped, along with images of himself. His clothes had been burned by his faithful servant, as per his specific directions, so there were no relics, but people satisfied themselves with his furniture and his books and other affects. Each of these became a focus of deification. His house had become a pilgrimage.

This saddened the Master. It was so much against everything he had taught. He then decided to visit 'his' kingdom a thousand years after his death. He found that the kingdom had been expanded in his name and innumerable brutalities had been committed coercing people to follow the 'Golden Word'.

He found that the 'Word' had become an idol. People had forgotten that it meant something, that once it had been a living thing, an active agent of change for the better. It had now become an instrument of coercion. There were differences in interpretation and each person with a different interpretation formed a sect around himself. He found one hundred and fifty such sects, each with its own version of the truth. He was saddened to note that none of these versions involved original thinking. They were just lexical manipulations of one sort or the other. He also found that every small thing he had done in his life – how he combed his hair, trimmed his beard, even how he scowled in mock anger at the children, had become an article of faith and those who did not adhere to it were persecuted as outcasts.

He remembered how he loved to laugh and to make his friends laugh. He found that all joy had gone out of the society of followers. It was as if laughter had been banned. He recalled how he used to encourage the womenfolk to advance. He found that the 'Word' had been used by menfolk as an instrument of suppression of women. He thought of how he wanted everyone to think for themselves – be creative and innovative. He found that all creativity had to conform to a rigid notion of what the 'Word' dictated.

He also found that the faithful were tinged with fear. This saddened him the most. His whole life had been lived in trying to free the people from fear, in trying to tell them that they were blessed by the divine, who was compassionate, and that there was no reason to fear him. Now, the people appeared fearful of everything. Every small transgression aroused feelings of deep guilt. They rushed to the priests to confess petty matters, and the priests were not above granting absolution for a consideration.

The people were so fearful even in taking his name – he did not know whether to laugh or cry at this – that they had made it a law that the words 'Bless him Almighty' must always follow his name. In the beginning he could not understand what they were saying – it was like a single word, an unbroken 'Holymasterblesshimalmighty'. He smiled when he could figure out what was being said and he burst out laughing when he saw what was being written. His written name had become 'Holy Master (BHA)'. Surely the faithful knew that the almighty had already blessed him and he did not need their intervention? What powers did they think they had which would make the almighty do their bidding? Shouldn't they be asking for themselves to be blessed, if at all?

The Master shook his head and decided to explore a bit more.

He discovered with some dismay that the essence of his teachings had been boiled down to praising the almighty day and night. Did they not understand that All-That-Is, which had created the universe, did not need to be reminded of its greatness by puny humans all the time? This was not why it had birthed humankind. Had it something like that in mind, a simple mirror would have sufficed. Humankind was sent on this plane to learn and progress so that it could be a part of nature-as-one.

The Master tried to discern why even the most intelligent followers had mortgaged their intelligence and were frittering away their time in 'buttering up' the almighty and the long-gone Master of Masters. They seemed to think that this conduct would lead them to some special favour in the eyes of the Lord, who would then give them the 'must-have' admission ticket for eternal 'heaven' where milk and honey will flow unabated, virgins would supposedly be available a-plenty and handsome, young men, too. This truly saddened the Master. It was so far from the truth and from common sense, too.

What was this heaven and hell they had invented? The Master had been careful not to show them visions of life after death. He always emphasized that they should live their life well; take care of their body and mind. He had taught them that if they lived a compassionate life through their hearts, the soul would be taken care of by itself. From old stories they seem to have resurrected this artificial and unverifiable mythical place where they wanted to spend their 'lives' after death? And the alternative was this ever-burning hell, where the compassionate almighty would subject them to all kinds of torture. He almost laughed at the inner contradiction – did they not realize that they were viewing the almighty as a shallow, vengeful, bribe accepting chief, something like their own leaders? How could they think that a compassionate lord, full of love and unity, would punish parts of himself this way and reward them if they kept praising him?

Apart from this, surely they realized that the pleasure and pain were a property of the mind and ceased to exist as soon as the brain died? Did they think that they would continue to wear this body in some sort of virtual imagery even after it had perished in earth or fire? Moreover, did they not realize that eternal bliss would pale before much time had elapsed and would become as boring as hell? He felt that one of the harshest punishments would be to condemn a person to repeat the same thing again and again. If someone was told to eat only sweet cake day and night, forever and ever, it would be a punishment made by the most cruel taskmaster.

He was sad to see that his followers seemed to have mortgaged the present to an uncertain future. Did they not understand that in order to accumulate their treasure for the future they had to take care of the present? And that this was to be done, not by chanting someone else's name and properties a hundred times a day, but by utilizing that time to create something worthwhile for society – by spreading love and goodwill, by alleviating poverty and ignorance and by creating happiness and fulfilment in other ways?

He shook his head, as if to remove unpleasant thoughts, and decided to see what the inside of a Ga'm now looked like. Unseen by the living, he entered the first one he came across. He saw that the entrance had a sign of crossed riding whips, ornately carved on the doors. Inside, the roof was a high vault-like structure, with rich wall-hangings. The 'Golden Word' was kept in a shrine, next to an ornate riding whip, with its handle made of what appeared to be solid gold. It was being worshipped by the followers, who asked it for blessings. The contents were being repeated ad-nauseum by acolytes who had remembered the words and forgotten the spirit. They, too, appeared joyless. However, he discovered a ray of unexpected light in all this gloom. He saw one of them silently hide the cap of another when the other one was busy in his recitals. He looked at the mischievous grin on this imp and grinned in empathy. He had done the same thing in his time. He silently blessed the young one and hoped that his spirit will not die under the yoke of his 'Word'. He knew, of course, that this was a vain hope. The 'Word' was too powerful.

With mild distress, he decided to visit the kingdom two thousand years after his death. He entered one of the most magnificent buildings in the kingdom, which now stretched all around the globe. As he expected, this was the Ga'm where one of the high priests presided. This personage was clothed in rich gold gowns, with a high peaked cap over his head. The cap had the same crossed whips in the centre. The Master smiled. The cap reminded him of a tea-cosy he used to have.

The high priest carried a golden riding whip in his hand. This puzzled the Master a bit, as had the ornate riding whip next to the 'Word' a thousand years earlier. He also noticed that all the priests, who lined the long and majestic corridor, had clothespins in the shape of the riding whips. Then he saw the small image of a horse and the coin dropped. The riding whip had become the symbol of authority of the priests. The horse was what would carry the faithful to heaven, as it was supposed to have carried the Master. He shook his head and smiled a bit sadly at the thought. Did they not know that he had never used a riding whip? He would just get on his favourite horse and think of the place where he wanted to go and the horse would take him there.

Unseen, he sat down in a pew and observed the ceremony going on. Apparently, some assistant high priests were being ordained. They appeared to be called Ga'mors. They entered the hall in single file, dressed in white smocks and had a simple white cloth tied on their heads. They carried simple riding whips in their hands, made of wood and hide. There was a light of righteousness in their eyes which made the master shudder. So, after two thousand years, 'rightness' becomes 'righteousness', he thought. He was pleased at the simple white gowns of the acolytes.

He listened to the oath these newly promoted Ga'mors had to take. The oath of poverty, chastity, honesty, humility. The oath of compassion. They drank a red liquid and pronounced words to the effect that it was the spirit of the Master they were imbibing. The Master did not know whether to laugh or cry.

Then they squeezed a sponge from which a thick blood-like fluid emerged and dropped in the basin below. They pronounced in a sing-song that this was the symbolic body of the unfaithful and they vowed to torture and exterminate all those who did not believe in the 'Word'.

Each was then blessed by a touch of the golden riding whip by the high priest and was given a gold ring with the 'holy' crossed riding whip symbol on it. Then they filed past a desk, where they were handed fine robes worked in much silver thread, not as grand as the high priest's but rich enough to glow in the light of the thousands of candles in the Ga'm. The newly anointed Ga'mors donned these robes, put on their new caps; again, not as high as the high priest's, but high enough. They handed in their simple riding whips and in exchange got silver ones. Now, fully attired and be-whipped, they bowed past the high priest again and sat down on the front row. The faithful present in the great hall applauded, and the media took moving and still pictures with cameras, which did not need film or much light.

The Master wondered how the irony of their oath could have escaped them. He also wondered what had happened to the 'Word'. If they professed to do as he had done, did they not remember that he had never worn a peaked cap or gown of gold? He saw the 'Word' sitting in great majesty on the central dais behind the high priest. The pages of this volume were at least ten feet long and six feet wide. It must weigh more than a ton, with its illuminated gold writing, he guessed. It lay there, theatrically open on its gold trellis support. Was it still his life story, he wondered? Did it still describe how he used to play tricks on his cousins? How he had embarrassed his uncle once, by making him wear shoes of different colours in the dark, before going out to meet a visiting dignitary? Did it list his simple food, his love for his one and only wife? How could this life story become this grand spectacle?

Depressed, he was going out when he had his answer. It struck him that his words and deeds had died when he had and had been cleverly embalmed by the well-meaning. Then they had been used by the self-serving. Like mummified remains, they had become increasingly fragile over time and the faithful had become increasingly militant in defending them.

He remembered noticing, a thousand years earlier, the concept of heresy arise its ugly head. He had seen people being sentenced to death for pronouncing a word incorrectly or for uttering a greeting which was supposed to be only the birthright of the faithful. He heard of one person sentenced to death because he had questioned whether the Master was really the son of a king. As if that mattered. In his lifetime thousands of people questioned this and the Master just laughed it off. Look at me for what I am, he had said, not whose son I am. Hear what I have to say, not what people say about me.

Learn from life – mine and yours and not through gossip. All this appeared so alive, then. His words shone and his deeds danced. But that was two thousand years back and, now, in this coffin-sized book, his words and deeds lay frozen, as if in a glamorous mortuary. High priests, no less, were the only ones allowed to interpret the 'Word'. All others had to abide by their diktat.

And that was not all. The Master discovered that there were at least four hundred high priests, each leading his own sect. Each interpreted the 'Word' in his own way. There were constant wars between these, each of whom maintained that they were the true spiritual descendants of the Master and all others were heretics.

One high priest was currently fighting another over the site on which both wanted to construct their Ga'm. Much violence, verbal and physical, was the result. All those who died were pronounced martyrs in some sort of holy war and were ensured an eternal heaven. All pleasures, most of which were physical, were promised to these martyrs by their priests.

It did not occur to the priests and other people that they were violating one of the most sacred and important truths of the almighty: 'Thou shalt love the living more than the dead.'

The Master shook his head. It seemed to him that he had been doing this a lot lately. What had happened to the brains of the faithful, he wondered. Surely, they should know that if they had been endowed with brains, these brains were meant to be used. His life and his words were simple enough for a child to understand. Alas, the power of indoctrination was so great that this simple idea could not be thought for fear of death, and children were not even allowed to touch a copy of the Word, lest they thoughtlessly defile it.

The Master did not have the heart to travel any further in time in 'his' kingdom. He did not wish to see what had become of his 'Word' when it had mummified further. With the power to travel where he wished, in any timeframe he wished, he decided to go away from this saddening spectacle altogether, in search of a world and a time where men and women lived in harmony amongst themselves and with nature, where mutual respect, love and compassion were the only words people respected and where people were free to use their questing hearts and brains to live a laughing, joyful, guiltless and fulfilling life.

And, where there were no Ga'ms and no priests.